Growing Up
As A
Greek-American

by
Dr. John L. Kallas

MISCHELE
WITH LOVE
FROM JOHN
WHO LOVES
YOU

**To my wife, Judith,
for her love, patience, and help**

KAV Books
First Avenue
Unionville, NY 10988
(914)726-3834
FAX: (914) 726-3824

ISBN: 0-88092-013-0

Printed in the United States of America by the Royal
Fireworks Press of Unionville, New York.

Table of Contents

Chapter One

Story Telling:
A Family Tradition

A Family Tradition

When Papa came to this country from Greece, he worked in Greek diners where he enjoyed philosophizing with the customers.

"In this country," he would say, "you judge a man by how much money he makes or by the kind of job he has. In my village, where there are no jobs and where no one has money, a man is judged by how well he can dance and how well he can tell a story."

While the four of us kids were growing up, Papa would tell us wonderful stories about the ancient Greek gods and goddesses, the Trojan War and the Odyssey. Like us, he heard these myths and stories from his father, who heard them in turn from his father. This family tradition of story telling goes back to the time of Homer.

Papa believed that a good story can capture the essence of an incident much better than a detailed factual account of what really happened.

Papa's Stories

We especially enjoyed Papa's stories about his experience in the Greek navy and how he fought the Turks during World War I. Here is a story that Papa told us many times. Each time he would tell it, he would alter it slightly, here and there, to give it a new twist or to improve the ending.

The Rescue
By Louis Kallas

When the first war broke out, I joined the Greek navy to fight the Turks. They made me a seaman on a small destroyer. Our captain was a *Vatikioti*. Everyone in the crew was a *Vatikioti*. We were afraid of nothing!

One day we got a radio message that a British aviator was shot down in Turkey over the Black Sea. He was still alive and our small destroyer was given the job of rescuing him.

The only way we could reach him was to go through the Bosphorous Strait. This was suicide! The Bosphorous Strait was less than a hundred feet wide with high cliffs and Turkish artillery on both sides.

As we slowly steamed up the Bosphorous, we could see the big Turkish guns on both sides pointing at us. They could have blown us out of the water, right then and there. But they didn't. They were laughing at us.

Our captain knew that the Turks were using the British aviator to bait us into a trap. They were playing with us, the way a cat plays with a mouse it has caught. On our way out, the Turks would blast us into a million pieces.

We found the aviator. He was badly wounded but still alive. When he opened his eyes and saw the Greek flag, he smiled and said, "Greek! Thank God." He then closed his eyes again.

We carried him aboard and headed back.

We dropped anchor just out of reach of the big guns and waited. There was a slight breeze blowing. I knew the captain had a plan in mind.

When the breeze died down, our captain gave the order to soak all our blankets, pillows, and sheets in black motor oil and then burn them!

Thick black smoke poured out of our smoke stack and drifted ashore towards the big guns.

He then gave us the orders to take off our clothes, underwear, socks, shoes, everything and soak them in oil and burn them too, and anything else we could soak in oil and burn.

Soon the entire sky was so black, you could not see your hand in front of you.

We quietly pulled up anchor and slipped by the Turks without them seeing us.

We were so close we could hear them coughing and cursing the smoke.

Hah hah hah! We burned everything! The only thing we did not soak in oil and burn was the Greek flag.

When we pulled into Cyprus to deliver the British aviator, we were all stark naked, including the captain and the aviator himself. We all stood at attention as they carried him off smiling.

Same Incident, Two Stories

Some of the best family stories were told by Mama and her sister, Aunt Mary. Here are their two stories of an incident that occurred during the Great Flu Epidemic of 1918.

Mama's Story:

I was 12 years old when I got the flu during the 1918 flu epidemic. The doctor told my mother that there was no hope of my getting better and that I would most likely die before daybreak.

Upon hearing this, my mother rushed out and bought me a new dress to be buried in.

It was the first time she ever bought me a new dress. (I always had to wear Mary's old dresses.)

Well, during the night my fever broke and the next morning, I was well again. My mother immediately went back to the store and got a refund on the new dress I never got to wear.

Aunt Mary's Story:

When Elsie (Mama) was sick with the flu and not expected to live through the night, our father sat on the front steps of our house with a loaded double-barrel shotgun.

A neighbor passed by and asked, *"Vrai Alkiviathie*, what are you doing sitting there with a shotgun?"

"I'm waiting for Charon. If that bastard comes here to take my *Ahlathaki* away, I'm going to blow his damn head off!"

Our father sat on those steps all night and the next morning, Elsie became well again. Charon did not show up.

(Note: In Ancient Greek mythology, Charon ferried dead souls across the River Styx. Today, many Greeks believe that Charon is Death himself.)

Papoo's Poetry

My mother's family came from The Mani, which is located in the lower Peloponnesus. The people who come from The Mani are called Maniates. The ability to create spontaneous poetry is relatively common with the Maniates. My *Papoo* (grandfather), who settled in Saco, Maine, had this uncanny ability.

This particular day in 1922 would have been like any other day in Saco if my *Papoo* hadn't been there to create a spontaneous poem about an incident that occurred in Kalayia's *Kafeneo* (Greek coffee house).

Mourmoura, a regular in the *kafeneo*, was sitting in his favorite chair, sipping his Greek coffee, when his dog strolled in and urinated on the *kafeneo's* spotless floor. A very angry Kalayia (the owner) grabbed his broom and chased both the dog and Mourmoura out of his *kafeneo*.

Before Kalayia put down his broom, my *Papoo* made up this four-line poem (translated):

Ol' Kalayia stands there with broom in hand,
Mourmoura from this place is forever banned.

Here, where no one is allowed even to spit,
Mourmoura's dog came in to do his bit.

Although this incident occurred seventy years ago, the Greeks in Saco still recite this poem as if it happened yesterday.

Voulas's Story

The family tradition of telling stories is alive and well in Greece. Each time we visit Greece, we are treated to many delightful stories about my mother and father when they lived there as children. Recently, our niece, Voula Haralambapoulos, sent me another family story about Papa.

I was visiting my aunts and grandmother in the Vatica this Christmas when my aunts told me this beautiful but sad story about your dad, Elias (Louis).

When your father, Elias, was a young boy, he used to sing a Greek folksong called, *Mia Voskopoula Ayapisa* (A Shepherdess, I Loved). It was his favorite song and he would always sit behind the church and sing it over and over again. All the people in the village knew that it was his special song.

Many years after he left the village to come to America these two old women were carrying water from the well to their homes in the village. As they walked by the church, they heard the song being sung by Elias.

When they reached the village, Elias's family had just received word from America that he had died. The two old women crossed themselves and told the rest of the villagers how they had just heard Elias singing his favorite song.

To this day, the villagers tell the story how the spirit of your dad had returned to his beloved village to sing his favorite song for the last time.

Chapter Two

The Greeks Come to America

Cold-Water Railroad Flats

The Greek families that settled in Newark, New Jersey during the early twenties lived within four blocks of each other on West Market Street. The houses they lived in were rows of old wooden tenements with one or two cold-water railroad flats on each floor.

These tenements were plentiful and cheap to rent because most people preferred to live in modern apartments that had hot water and central heating. Most of our parents came from small mountain villages that had no running water, gas, or electricity. Every drop of water had to be carried home in large tin cans filled at the village well. So, the tenements in Newark were a luxury by comparison. After all, they did have gas, electricity, running water, and indoor bathrooms. What more could anyone ask for?

The apartments were called railroad flats because the rooms were laid out in a straight row. The parlor was located in the front of the house, the large kitchen in the back, with two bedrooms in between. During the cold winter months, the front parlor was kept closed, and the children slept in the warmest bedroom next to the kitchen.

In the winter, our lives centered around the huge hot coal stove located in the kitchen. *Hestia*, the gentle goddess of the hearth, smiled down on us as we sat around that stove roasting chestnuts, drying our wet sneakers in the oven, and telling stories.

It was my job to keep the coal bucket full and to provide the stove with the endless supply of firewood needed to boost the burning of the large chunks of black coal.

In Greece, the children would scour the mountainside for dead branches and broken twigs. In Newark, we were always on the lookout for discarded wooden boxes or crates.

Whenever we spotted one, we would drag it home and break it into pieces small enough to fit into the stove. (To this day, when I pass a wooden box or a crate, I get this tremendous urge to drag it home.)

Mama used our hot coal stove with great skill. There were always three or four pots simmering on top and the sweet smell of Greek bread baking in the oven.

No matter how busy Mama was, she always found time to talk to Kyria Georgina, who lived next door. Each morning, after we kids went to school, Kyria Georgina would open her window and call out to my mother, *"Ahlayia!"* (*Ahlayia* is my mother's name in Greek.) Mama had no trouble hearing Kyria Georgina's loud high-pitched voice.

Mama would open her window and the conversation that followed usually lasted for an hour. They talked about what they were going to cook for dinner, any medical problems they were having, the latest gossip, etc., etc., etc.!

One morning, Mama was washing the breakfast dishes when she heard Kyria Georgina calling, *"Ahlayia!"*

Mama opened her window as she always did; however, Kyria Georgina was not there. As a matter of fact, her window was closed.

So, Mama went back to washing her dishes. A few minutes went by, when she heard Kyria Georgina calling her again, *"Ahlayia!"* Again, Mama opened her window and saw no Kyria Georgina. Just a closed window. This time, she was a bit puzzled by what was happening.

When it happened a third time, Mama was steaming mad. She stormed next door and banged on Kyria Georgina's door.

When Kyria Georgina opened her door, she was surprised to see my mother. She was even more surprised when my mother blasted her.

"You may think your little joke is funny, but I don't!"

"Ahlayia, I don't know what you're talking about!"

"Don't give me that! You know damn well what I'm talking about!"

At that precise moment, someone in the backyard interrupted my mother's tirade by calling out, *"Ahlayia!"* in a loud, high-pitched voice.

Both women rushed into the kitchen and opened the window! Again, they heard, *Ahlayia!*

My mother called back, "I'm *Ahlayia!* Who are you? What do you want?"

Ahlayia! Ahlayia! Caw! Caw!

That's when it dawned on Mama that the voice was that of a parrot kept in a cage on a neighbor's back porch.

Ahlayia! Ahlayia! Caw! Caw!

A perfect imitation of Kyria Georgina's loud, high-pitched voice.

Many people referred to neighborhoods like West Market Street as *Greek ghettos.* However, those of us who grew up in them don't quite see it that way. These neighborhoods provided us with fond memories and a source for many stories describing what it was like growing up as Greek-Americans.

The Matter of Birth Certificates

I was born on August 3rd, 1922. At least that's what I was led to believe until my ninety-one-year-old Aunt Mary recently informed me that I was not born on August 3rd. I was born on August 15th.

"I remember it well," she said to me. "You were born on *Panayia's*, which always falls on August 15th." Although she remembered the month and the day, she could not remember the exact year I was born. And there's no way I can find out because I don't have a birth certificate. My sister, Helen, and my brother, Constantine, don't have birth certificates either. We were brought into this world by *Yria Levakina*, the village midwife, who came to America with my parents in 1920.

In those days, thousands of children were born to immigrants without the benefit of birth certificates. It was much too complicated to deal with the bureaucracy at City Hall (no one there understood Greek). Besides, there was no need for a birth certificate since we celebrate our name days and not our birthdays. It's a much easier system.

I get dozens of calls on St. John's Day from my relatives and Greek friends, wishing me a long life and good health. Hardly anyone ever calls me on August 3rd to wish me a happy birthday.

To this day, Greek mothers determine their children's relative age in the following manner: "Your Niko is two years older than my Eleni because he was walking while I was still breast-feeding Eleni."

However, our parents didn't realize how often we would be asked to provide proof of our exact age.

In this country, your age determines when you can start school, get a driver's license, enlist in the army, drink beer, see an R rated movie, buy cigarettes, vote, obtain a credit card, get a job, get married, retire, collect Social Security, and receive Medicare payments.

Thank goodness, when the time came for me to prove my age, the authorities agreed to accept an affidavit (in lieu of a birth certificate) from my mother claiming that I was born on a certain day. She knew this to be true, because she was there when I was born.

13

My brother, Babe, was the only one in our family to have a genuine birth certificate since he was the only one born in a hospital. All hospitals automatically provide city clerks with birth certificates of newly born infants.

Incidentally, we called my brother "Babe" because he was the baby of the family, and it was three years before he was baptized and given our grandfather's name, "Alkiviades," which somehow was translated to "Archie."

Babe hated the name "Archie," especially when he went to school, where the kids called him "Archie-bald." When he complained about it to my mother, she would say to him, "You should be very proud of your name. It was my father's name and the name of a great general who fought in the ancient Peloponessian wars!"

Well, the time came in 1946, when Babe needed to provide proof of his age to the draft board. He promptly went to the Hall of Records in Newark and asked for a copy of his birth certificate.

"Miss," he politely said to the clerk, "My name is Archie Kallas. I was born on July 18th, 1928, and I would like to have a copy of my birth certificate."

The clerk smiled and checked the files (they didn't have computers in those days).

"I'm sorry," she said, "but we don't have any record of an Archie Kallas born on that day."

"Oh no!" Babe cried, "Please don't say that. It has to be there. I'm the only one in my family that has a birth certificate."

"Well, let me look some more." She continued searching through the files.

"Ahh! Here's a Thomas Kallas born on June 12th, 1928."

"What's the name of the parents?" Babe asked.

"Elsie and Louis Kallas."

"That's me!" he exclaimed

Babe rushed home with his birth certificate and immediately confronted my mother.

"Ma! what's my name?" he asked.

14

"Why do you ask such a stupid question? Your name is Alkiviades and you should be proud of that name. It was my father's name and…"

Babe wouldn't let her finish. "Then how come my birth certificate says my name is Thomas?"

Babe handed Mama his birth certificate. She studied it for a few moments, thought back, and suddenly remembered.

"Ahh! Now, I remember! It was in the hospital. The nurse asked me what we were going to name you and I told her Thomas. That's right! We were going to name you after my brother *Thoma*!"

"And another thing." Babe was relentless. "When's my birthday?"

"We always celebrate your birthday on July 18th. Why?"

"My birth certificate says I was born on June 12th."

Mama handed Babe his birth certificate and said, "Well, you can't expect me to remember everything! Now, go wash your hands and set the table for dinner."

Greek Christmas

The most joyous time for us Greek kids living in Newark, New Jersey was Christmas, which we celebrated the way our parents did in their mountain villages in Greece.

On Christmas Day, our neighborhood became alive with the singing of small groups of Greek carolers. They would go from floor to floor in each tenement singing the Greek equivalent of carols: the *Kallanda*.

The carolers would always end their singing by wishing everyone good health and long life. We would respond by offering them token gifts of small coins, *koulourakia*, tangerines, chestnuts or dried figs. The carolers would then move on to the next floor.

One year, a group of carolers asked me to join them. I became so excited, I lost my voice. So, they gave me a small metal triangle and gently told me to accompany them, while they did the singing.

The celebration of Greek Christmas lasts twelve days, from Christmas to the Epiphany. Although these twelve days are filled with delightful songs, feasts and celebrations, they are also filled with fear and terror, because of the horrible *Kallikantsaroi* who were out there, causing all sorts of mischief during this period.

Before falling asleep at night, I took great joy in frightening my two younger brothers and sister with horror stories about the *Kallikantsaroi*.

"What are *Kallikantsaroi?*," Helen would ask.

"They are goblins and evil spirits!"

"Did you ever see one?"

"Many times. As a matter of fact, I saw two this morning and one about an hour ago."

"You did? Wow!" Babe, the youngest one, cried out.

Constantine, the skeptic, would challenge me, "**Oh Yeah?** Then tell us what they looked like!"

I was ready for him.

"Well, to begin with, all three were goblins. One had horns, a long pointed tail, and one eye in the middle of its forehead; the other had bright red eyes and a huge ugly scar across its face; and the one I saw an hour ago had the legs of a goat and arms of a monkey."

16

"Do they eat people?"

"Naw...just rotten vegetables and squiggly worms."

"Where do they come from?"

Mama would then step in and say, "They come from the bowels of the earth! Now, be quiet and go to sleep!"

Papa didn't believe in the *Kallikantsaroi*. Mama, however, took their existence quite seriously. She believed that any child born on Christmas would turn into one The only way to prevent this from happening was to bind the newborn infant with garlic tresses or straw.

Then again, Mama believed in a lot of things, especially during the Twelve Days of Christmas. For example, she would warn us to never, **never** cry on New Year's Day, because if we did, we would spend the entire year crying.

Papa believed in other things. He would play cards on New Year's Eve and continue to play well past midnight to find out how *Chance* was going to treat us in the coming year.

Of course, if you were given the slice of the New Year's Day *Vasilopitta* with the magic coin imbedded in it, you were guaranteed good luck for the rest of the year, regardless of how Papa made out in his card game the night before.

Celebrating Greek Christmas enriched our lives because as children, we shared the same experiences our parents had when they were children in their small mountain villages in Greece.

It only lasted a short time before we grew up and became Americanized.

But, that's another story.

Chapter Three

Childhood

Shopping with Mama

When I was six years old, my mother insisted on dragging me along when she went shopping. "I need you to translate!" she told me.

Mama had no trouble communicating with the sales people. No matter where she was or what she was buying, she would ask, "How much?"

The salesperson would say "Two-ninety-five."

I would close my eyes, because I knew what was coming next.

"Too much!" my mother would say. "I give you two dollars."

"Ma," I would whisper in Greek, "you can't do that here. This is *Bambergers.*"

The salesperson would smile and gently say, "I'm sorry, but we're not allowed to do that sort of thing here," and politely put the merchandise back on the shelf.

"*Ti eipe?* What did she say?" Mama would ask.

"She said, no sale, Ma." I would pull her by the hand, "so, let's go."

Although she had no success with the large department stores, she did much better bargaining in the small retail stores. Somehow, my mother discovered that some small retail merchants believed that losing the first sale of the day would bring bad luck for the rest of the day. Mama would take me along early in the morning and hit two or three stores as they opened.

"How much?"

"Three-fifty."

"Too much!"

My mother would turn and head for the door, dragging me behind her.

"Lady! Wait!" the merchant would call out, "I'll give it to you for three-twenty-five."

Mama would stop in her tracks and say, "Too much!"

"All right," the merchant would say, "take it for three dollars."

I knew then that Mama had her fish hooked. She would return to the merchant, look at him straight in the eye, and say, "One dollar."

The merchant would look at her in total disbelief, "Madame, are you crazy? It cost me twice that to buy it wholesale."

Mama didn't bother to ask me to translate. "One dollar!"

Out of desperation, the merchant would turn to me and say, "Sonny, talk to your mother. Tell her to be reasonable."

I would simply shrug my shoulders.

"One dollar!" My mother was relentless.

After haggling, for what seemed like hours, the poor merchant would finally give in, give the merchandise to Mama, and take the dollar.

My mother beamed with pride as she walked out of the store. Whereas, I felt totally embarrassed, humiliated, and guilty.

All this happened sixty-five years ago. Recently, I spent Christmas with my sister in Maine. I didn't know what gifts to buy for her grandchildren, so she took me to a huge toy discount store. The store was practically empty, because of the terrible recession. My sister found a toy kitchen set discounted 60 percent. It was exactly what her granddaughter wanted. I then watched my sister take the box to the store manager. She told him that the box was slightly damaged, and she wanted an additional 20 percent off.

"Look!" she said, "Tomorrow is Christmas and your store is empty. This is your only chance to get rid of this damaged box."

The manager looked at me. I shrugged my shoulders.

"Yes 'mam. Just tell the cashier that Frank said it was okay to give you an additional 20 percent off on this."

"My God," I thought, "it must be in our blood."

The Canaries

Papa was a dreamer and as kids, we shared his wonderful dreams. "Someday when we become rich," he would say, "we will buy our own boat." The next day, we would search through old magazines and cut out pictures of boats to show him when he came home from work.

He was the eternal optimist. As far as he was concerned, anything was possible. One day, he came home from work with an idea of how we could make a lot of money.

"How Papa? Tell us how!" We were all very excited.

"Canaries!"

"Canaries?"

He had it all figured out. We gathered around him at the kitchen table as he sketched out his plan.

"First, we begin with two canaries, a boy and a girl."

"Two canaries." We echoed.

"These two canaries will get together and lay two eggs."

"Just like the chickens do," I added.

"*Bravo Yiannaki.* The two eggs will hatch and we will have four canaries instead of two. And the four canaries will get together and make eight canaries, and the eight will make sixteen, and so on, and so on."

"Wow!"

"Where will we keep all these birds?" Mama, the realist, asked.

"In the small front room," Papa responded with a smile.

"Yeah! The small front room!" we shouted, in support of Papa.

"Good!" Papa announced, "Tomorrow, I will bring home the two birds."

The next day, my sister, Helen, and I hiked five miles to Branchbrook Park, ripped dozens of branches from the trees, lugged them back to Richmond Street, and nailed them onto the walls of the small front room. Meanwhile, my smaller brothers, Constantine and Babe, scattered cotton, thread, and strips of paper that the birds could use to build their nest.

22

That evening, we all waited at the bus stop for Papa. Sure enough, Papa was carrying a small white box when he got off the bus.

"Here they are!" he laughed, holding the box up over his head.

"Hurrah!" we shouted as we walked home. Papa handed me the box and picked up Babe, who was too small to keep up with us. The box had tiny holes punched in it, and I could hear the canaries inside chirping. They were as excited as we were.

Papa was pleased with the way we had fixed the room. The only thing he had to do was cover the window with a bed sheet so the canaries wouldn't smash their heads against the window attempting to fly out. When he released them from the small box, they flew around the room and eventually landed on one of the branches, chirping to each other.

"What are they saying?" Babe asked.

"They like it here," Helen squealed with delight.

"Alright, let's leave them alone," Papa said.

Questions and speculation abounded while eating supper. As usual, everyone was talking at the same time.

"Is one a boy and the other a girl bird?"

"Of course dummy. How else can they make baby birds?"

"How can we be sure?"

"When will they lay their first eggs?"

"They have to first build a nest."

"How long will that take?"

"I dunno!"

Well, we didn't have to wait too long. The canaries immediately started to build their nest and within a week, we discovered two, small, light blue speckled eggs in it.

God, those were exciting days. Each evening, we would greet Papa at the bus stop with the latest news.

A few days after the eggs were laid, we met Papa with tears in our eyes.

"What's wrong?" Papa asked.

"Someone broke the eggs," we cried.

"Who would do a thing like that?"

"We don't know, Papa. They were broken when we came home from school."

Stunned, sad, and puzzled, we cleaned out the nest.

That evening we quietly ate our supper. The silence was broken by the loud sounds of fire engine sirens stopping in front of our house. We rushed to the living room and saw flames shooting out of the house across the street. We opened the windows and watched the firemen fighting the fire. It was all very interesting until we saw Babe's head sticking out of the window in the birds' room.

"The birds! The birds!" we shouted as we rushed into the small front room. But it was too late. The two canaries had already flown out the window.

Forty years later, I found out who had broken the two eggs. I stumbled across a government pamphlet on *How to Raise Canaries.* It explained that the male bird must be separated from the female while she is hatching her eggs. Otherwise, the male bird will peck at the eggs until they are broken.

"Had we known, we could have made millions, Papa."

The Easter Candle

The way we Greek kids celebrated Easter was totally different from the way American kids celebrated theirs. Their parents deluged them with Easter baskets filled with straw, colored jelly beans, chocolate rabbits, and marshmallow baby chicks.

Our parents celebrated Easter the same way they had in their villages. For forty days they didn't eat meat, fish, chicken or any food that contained milk, butter, eggs, lard or any ingredient that came from an animal. We kids were required to fast for one week only.

On the Saturday night before Easter, Papa took us to church. Mama stayed home to put the final touches on the feast we were to have when we returned, usually around one o'clock in the morning.

Before entering the church, Papa bought us each a *lambatha*, a huge white candle. The Easter church services were always magnificent and filled with pathos and drama. They were psychologically timed to elevate us to sheer ecstasy at 12 midnight, the precise moment of Christ's resurrection. That's when all the lights would go out, leaving the church in total darkness. The priest would sing out *"Xristos Anestti!"* as he lit his candle from the *candillie* hanging above the altar and pass the flame down to the people sitting up front. From there the lit candles multiplied and within moments the church was ablaze with lit candles and people joyfully crying, *"Xristos Anestti!"* (Christ has risen!) *"Alithios Anestti!"* (He has truly risen!)

In the villages, the people would bring back the lit candle and light the *candillie* that hung in their homes. They believed, as did our parents that the flame was blessed and would protect the family in the coming year.

The task of bringing home the lit candle fell on my shoulders, since I was the oldest son and had always succeeded in years past.

However, bringing home a lit candle in the village was a lot easier than bringing one home in Newark, where you had to walk three long blocks to the bus stop, take a bus, and then walk six blocks to your house.

It was especially difficult if it was snowing or raining with a strong wind blowing, which was exactly what it was doing this one Easter. Papa and the kids went home ahead of me because I had to walk very slowly to the bus while holding the lit candle under my coat. The cold rain was relentless. The water seeped through my coat, my suit, and finally through my underwear.

When I reached the bus stop, I stood in the rain for what seemed like hours before the bus finally came. The few people on the bus thought I was crazy and laughed as they watched me struggle to dig a nickel out of my wet pocket and toss it into the coin receptacle without letting the lit candle go out.

When I got off the bus, the rain had turned to sleet, and the sidewalks to slabs of solid ice making my six block trek a treacherous one. The wind continued to slice through me, and my wet clothes started to freeze.

Finally, I reached our apartment building. As I entered into the hallway, I opened my coat ever so slightly to check the candle. It was still glowing. Wham! The door slammed shut and pooof...the candle went out!

Everyone upstairs was singing and celebrating. I could hear Papa laughing.

"Don't worry, our Yianni will bring home the lit candle!"

Holding the smoking candle in my hand, I didn't know what to do. I didn't know what to tell them. I put my frozen hand into my wet pocket, and there it was! A book of dry matches. I didn't waste any time lighting the candle and opening the door to our apartment.

Everyone cheered when they saw me standing there with the lit candle. *"Bravo Yianni!"* Papa shouted. Mama took the candle, crossed herself, and lit the *candillie* with it. *"Ach! Yiannaki mou."* She smiled as she kissed me, "The holy flame will protect us and bring us good fortune for the coming year."

The coming year was one that I will never forget. I had sinned and God was sure to punish me by harming my younger sister or brothers. For the entire year I didn't let them out of my sight.

The year went by and, aside from getting the measles, nothing happened to them. The way I see it now, a miracle occurred that night. Where did those matches come from? And how did they remain dry enough for me to light the candle?

It was a miracle.

The First Greek-American Telephone

In the early thirties, the Greeks, who lived in Newark had no need for a telephone, since they all lived within four blocks of each other. Any communication with the outside world was done through the pay phone in Mrs. Katz's candy store. Relatives living anywhere in the world could reach us in an emergency by calling Mrs. Katz's.

All this changed when Olga Boucouvalas graduated Normal School with a degree in education. She needed a telephone to receive calls in the afternoon from schools that needed a substitute the next morning.

Thus the telephone company installed the first telephone ever owned by a Greek family in Newark. It was a modern, early thirties all-black model, that stood vertical on a round base, with the earpiece hanging along its side. The telephone was placed in the center of the kitchen table. Each afternoon, the neighborhood children would sit around that table, staring at the telephone for hours, waiting for it to ring. If they were lucky, the phone would ring. When this happened, they jumped in their chairs and screamed

"Olga! Olga! The telephone! The telephone!"

They immediately quieted down when Olga came in and answered the telephone in the most dignified manner, "Hello?"

A slight giggle surfaced as Olga listened to someone on the other end.

"Yes, this is Olga Boucouvalas."

Another pause and a few more hushed giggles.

"Room 215. Yes, I will be there. 8 o'clock tomorrow morning. Thank you for calling. Goodbye."

When Olga hung up, the children screamed with delight. They had just witnessed the miracle of telecommunications. The children would eventually quiet down and take their places around the table again, staring at the telephone, waiting for another miracle to happen.

Melting Ice

In the early thirties, Greek families in Newark were extremely proud of their American iceboxes. Great care was given to keep the ice in these iceboxes from melting too soon.

They covered the ice with heavy towels and opened the icebox door as little as possible. But alas, no matter what they did, on a hot summer day the ice would melt and fill the large pan under the icebox with water in less than three hours.

Our entire social life was restricted by this three-hour time span. When we went out to visit one of our Greek relatives, we would empty the pan and check the clock before leaving. We had to make sure to return in time to empty the pan before it overflowed.

Great skill was required to pull out a full pan of water from under the icebox, lift it up from the floor, carry it to the sink, and empty it without spilling any water on the floor.

I was eleven years old when I resolved this problem. Using a rock and a large nail, I punched a hole through the kitchen wall facing the alley next to the house. I pushed a portion of a small red hose through the hole in the wall and attached the other end to the pipe sticking out from beneath the icebox. I immediately ran down the three flights of stairs and into the alley. I looked up and saw my red hose sticking out. Drip! Drip! Drip! It was dripping water!

I waited outside for Papa to come from work. He smiled when he saw me running down the street to greet him.

"Papa! Papa! Come with me! I want to show you something!"

I led him into the alley way and pointed to my little red rubber hose sticking out the wall, three stories up.

My father looked up, "What is it?"

"It's dripping water, see!" I said pointing to a puddle of water that had formed on the ground.

"Where is it coming from?" Papa asked.

"From our icebox, Papa! I fixed it so we never have to empty that stupid water pan ever again!"

My father picked me up and hugged me.

"*Bravo Yiannaki mou!* You are truly a genius!"

A genius? Wow!

I Mixed My Blood With
The Devil's Blood

My mother always dreamed that her first son would become a priest like her brother, Papa Leonidas. It was a Kyriakakos tradition for the oldest son in each family to be a priest. However, when I was born, my father immediately rejected the idea that I become a priest. From that day on, my mother suspected my father of being the devil, himself. Each morning, she would cross herself and pray, "Forgive me God, for I have mixed my blood with the devil's blood."

She was especially worried that something terrible would happen on the day I was to be baptized. But much to her surprise, everything went off like clockwork. The priest had my Godfather open the front door of the church and spit outdoors to keep out any evil spirits. My mother handed my tiny naked body to the priest who dabbed olive oil on my forehead and chanted, "May you always have God in your thoughts." He continued to chant as he covered my entire body with thick green olive oil.

The priest then dunked me into a huge tub of ice cold water. He held my head underwater and he chanted some more. I screamed in terror when he let me come up for air. My mother smiled when she heard my screams. She was sure that the evil spirits were being purged from my body. When the priest pushed my head under for a second time, my mother crossed herself and thanked God for purifying my soul.

Although my mother's fears had subsided somewhat after the baptism, she continued to have nightmares about me being possessed by the devil. I was ten years old when her worst nightmare became a reality.

It happened on the morning of Holy Saturday in 1932. I went to church to *metalavi* (receive communion) with all the other Greek children in Newark. We were not allowed to eat or drink anything that morning before receiving communion, so we were all anxious to get this over with as quickly as possible. The one who was most anxious to finish quickly was our ill-tempered priest, Father Papaspyridakis. Facing a line of over two hundred restless kids, he was close to the edge.

When my turn finally came, I did everything I was supposed to do. I kissed the priest's golden ring as he mumbled something I did not understand. I opened my mouth as wide as I could and gulped down the holy wine the priest doled out with a tiny gold spoon. I was very careful not to let any wine spill on the floor because if I did, I would have to get on my hands and knees and lick the holy wine off the floor.

Whew! Finished at last! Now, I can go home and get something to eat, I thought as I lightly wiped my lips with holy cloth draped over the priest's arm.

That's when it happened! For no apparent reason, Father Papaspyridakis glared down at me and snarled, *"Vrai diavolai!"* (You devil!)

Without thinking, I responded, *"Na se pari!"* (He should take you!)

When he heard what I said, the priest fell back in disbelief. Everyone in the church was shocked.

"Johnnie Kallas just told the priest to go to hell!" they whispered.

"What? Here in church?"

"Yes! And on the holiest of holy days!"

The priest quickly recovered. *"Cataremenai!"* (Cursed one!) he cried out. He then ordered me out of the church and told me never to set foot in it again.

Everyone crossed themselves and stepped back as I walked by them on my way out.

Nick Marcus, my best friend who was behind me, soon came out.

"What made him blow his top like that?" I asked.

"Dummy, you wiped your lips with the yellow side of the holy cloth instead of the red side."

"Oh...oh! I better get home before my mother hears about this!"

"C'mon, I'll race you!" Nick yelled and took off.

I was much faster than Nick, so I reached our block ahead of him. I rushed up the stairs of our tenement building and by the time I reached the second floor, I knew my mother had heard the news. I smelled the sandlewood burning in the *thimiato* (an incense burner hanging from three heavy chains). I also heard my mother praying as she filled the house and the hallway with the holy smoke pouring out of the *thimiato*.

When my mother saw me standing at the doorway, she let out a bloodcurdling scream, "AGHH! There is the devil's son who told the priest to go to hell on the holiest of holy days!"

While she was screaming, she kept swinging the *thimiato* by its heavy chains over her head, around and around, faster and faster.

"Aw, Ma."

"Don't call me Ma!" And after a final bloodcurdling scream, she let go of the *thimiato*. It went sailing across the room at one hundred miles an hour. BAM! It hit me on the head and knocked me to the floor. I touched my forehead and felt warm blood oozing out. I looked up and saw Mama coming towards me with blood in her eyes. I quickly got to my feet and ran down the stairs before she could reach me. I could see that Mama was in no mood to feed me, so I went next door to Thea Boucouvalina to get something to eat. Thea Boucouvalina, my favorite aunt, was the kindest and most gentle person in the universe. She was always cooking and would never let me go hungry.

When Thea Boucouvalina saw me, she stood in front of her six children and held her arms out as if to protect them from me.

"Please Yianni." Her voice trembled with fear, "Do not hurt my children. Please go away."

I received the same treatment from all the Greeks in the neighborhood.

The only thing left for me to do was to wait for Papa to come home from work, so, I hid behind the stairwell outside our apartment. Finally, I heard Papa coming up the stairs. As usual, he ran up the stairs two steps at a time. When he reached our floor, I stepped out of my hiding place and greeted him.

"Hello, Papa."

That's when he saw the dried blood on my forehead.

"What the hell happened to you?"

Before I could answer, he opened the door and yelled, "Hey! What the hell happened to *Yianni!*"

When my mother saw him, she screamed, "Aaaagh! There's the devil himself with his cursed offspring!" and reached for her *thimiato,* which was still smoking.

"Oh oh!" I grabbed my father by the arm, "C'mon Papa, we better get out of here, fast!"

A Matter of Taste

Papa did many things and did them well in his short lifetime. As a young man he was a fisherman. When Greece entered World War I, Papa joined the Greek navy and served as a seaman aboard a destroyer. After the war he became a merchant seaman in the Greek maritime fleet and later came to America and worked in the cotton mill factories in Maine.

He then joined his brothers in the Colorado coal mines and dug coal for three years. Papa left the Colorado coal mines and settled in Newark, New Jersey, where the only work he could find was washing dishes in a small coffee shop owned by his cousin.

Soon he became a short-order cook working at lightning speed during rush hours filling the orders screamed in to him by the waitresses.

"BLT, down! Hold the mayo!"

"Two over, light!"

"Adam and Eve on a raft!"

In time, he learned to cook and became a chef. In fifteen years he elevated himself from a dishwasher to a first-class chef with a tall, fancy white chef's hat, and he worked in the kitchens of the most elegant restaurants and hotels.

He was surrounded by the most expensive food imaginable: live lobsters flown in from Maine, jumbo shrimps from Florida, and the choicest cuts of meat. Even though he had a wide range of food to eat, he always chose to eat at home.

When he came home, he would sit down at the table and eat fried white fish marinated in vinegar, goat's cheese, and bitter black olives. He would dip his hard Greek bread into a glass of homemade wine, slice raw onions into a bowl of yellow fava puree, and pour green virgin olive oil over some over-cooked dandelions.

When he finished eating, Papa would gulp down another glass of wine, push back his chair, pat his stomach with both hands, and say, "Ahhh! Now, *that's* what I call a meal!"

Chapter Four

School Years

The Spit Story

Many Greeks will often spit to express their feelings. For example, in the final chapter of *Eleni*, Nicholas Gage spits in the face of the man he believes killed his mother.

We all know that the surest way to keep the evil eye away is to spit, *"Ptoo! Na mei poskathie!"*

Well, this form of expression got me into deep trouble with Miss Keys, my third grade teacher. It happened one day when she had us read to ourselves in class. Billy... Goat... Gruff... was... crossing... the.. bridge... (I was a slow reader) "when... the... ugly... troll... jumped... out... from... under... the... bridge... and... ate... Billy.. Goat... Gruff!

The troll ate Billy Goat Gruff? I was horrified.

When I saw the sketch in the book of the ugly troll, my horror turned into outrage. I naturally spit, *"Ptoo!* Bad troll!"

At that precise moment, Miss Keys was walking by my desk and saw me spitting in my book.

"Aaaaagh!" she screamed. Much to my surprise, she grabbed me by my ear, pulled me out of my chair, and into the hallway.

"You filthy boy! You go home and bring your mother here immediately!"

I was dumbfounded. "Why?" I asked.

"Go! Go!" she screamed, "I want to see your mother. Now! "

So, I headed home. I didn't know what to tell my mother, since I didn't know why Miss Keys was so upset.

When I got home, my mother was surprised to see me.

"Vrai, what are you doing home from school so early?" she asked.

"My teacher, Miss Keys, wants to see you right away."

"Right away? What for?"

"I don't know, Ma. She said I did something filthy."

My mother's mood suddenly changed, "What the hell did you do?

"I didn't do anything, I swear!"

My mother combed her hair, put on her hat and in a matter of minutes, we were on our way to school. My mother continued to question me as she dragged me along.

"Did you show your *companella* in class?"

"Of course not, Ma!" I was quite indignant.

"You didn't pee in class, did you?"

"Oh Ma!" More indignation.

"You must have done something terrible. Why would she send you home?"

"I really don't know, Ma."

We finally reached the school. Miss Keys was sitting on a bench in the hallway still in shock and taking smelling salts.

Oh Mrs. Kallas! I'm so glad you came. She cried, "You will never believe what your son did in my class."

"What... What did he do?"

"In all my years of teaching, I have never encountered anything so filthy!"

"*Po... Po... po...*" My mother expected the worst as she looked at me with fire in her eyes. I shrugged my shoulders.

"Please, Miss Keys. Tell me. What did he do?" My mother pleaded.

"I can't bring myself to say it."

"You must tell me. How else can I punish him?"

"All right, I will tell you." Miss Keys covered her eyes. "Your son spit in his book."

My mother was so relieved, she started to smile. Miss Keys peaked through her fingers to see what my mother was going to do. My mother spotted this and took the cue.

She turned to me, "*Vrai!* Did you spit in your book? *Ptoo!* You bad boy!"

I saw the spit coming and ducked. It went over my head and hit Miss Keys head-on instead.

Poor Miss Keys.

The Christmas Tree

I was in the third grade when I learned about exchanging Christmas presents. After decorating the Christmas tree in our classroom, the teacher told us to bring a Christmas present to class and put it under the tree. She also told us not to spend more than ten cents on the present. When I came home that day, I immediately told my mother I needed ten cents for school.

"What for?" she asked.

"To buy a present to put under the Christmas tree in our classroom."

"A Christmas tree?" she asked.

"It's a tree we decorate to celebrate the birth of Christ. Each class decorates one. The principal is going to give a prize for the one that's decorated the best."

"*Po..po..po!* You're going too fast for me. Why do you need the ten cents?"

"Mama, I already told you. To buy a gift, to put under the Christmas tree."

"And who is this gift for?"

"I don't know, Mama. On the last day of school we are going to have a Christmas party, and each kid is going to pick a present from under the tree without knowing who it's from."

"Then how do you know what to buy?"

"Mama, it's not important what you buy or who gets it. The teacher said what matters is the idea of giving and receiving at Christmas."

"If I give you a dime, what will you buy with it?"

"The harmonica that's in Mrs. Katz's candy store window. I'll also need an extra penny to buy Christmas paper to wrap it in."

"I'll think about it."

"But Mama, there's nothing to think about. I don't want to be the only one in class not bringing in a present."

"I said, I'll think about it. Now, change your clothes and do your homework."

I wasn't worried. We still had a week before Christmas and I was sure Mama would give me the money.

Life for Mama became more complicated the next day when my sister, Helen, came home from school with a picture she drew in her second grade class. She loved to draw and was anxious to show her latest picture to Ma.

"Mama, look at what I drew in class today"

"Hmmm, nice. Very nice." She was a bit puzzled by it.

"It's a picture of Santa Claus!"

"Santa Claus?"

I saw that Mama didn't know who Santa Claus was. So, I jumped in, "He lives at the North Pole with his wife and a bunch of elves!"

Helen proudly pointed to her picture, "I put them in the picture too. See?"

I pressed ahead, "On Christmas eve, he brings toys and presents to children all over the world."

Mama looked at the picture again. "How does he do that?"

Helen pushed me aside. "He has a sled and reindeer that fly. He lands on the roof and comes down the chimney."

Mama handed the picture back to Helen.

"Is that what they teach you in school?"

"No Mama. It's what all the kids talk about. Santa Claus and what toys he's going to bring them."

"The kids in my class write him letters, telling him what they want for Christmas."

As usual, Constantine was skeptical. "Well, I don't believe in Santa Claus!"

"I do."

"So do I."

"Me too!" Babe, the youngest, joined in.

"Then how come he doesn't land on our roof and bring us presents?"

"Maybe, he doesn't like Greek kids."

"Naw! He loves all kids."

"I know why."

They all focused their attention on me.

"Because we don't have a Christmas tree."

"Papa will never buy one."

"Not in a million years"

"Alright!" Mama brought us back to reality. "All of you, change your clothes and start your homework!"

Of course, Mama eventually gave me the money to buy the harmonica. I wrapped it up with bright colored Christmas paper, brought it to school and put it under the Christmas tree.

On the last day of school, we had our Christmas party. The harmonica I bought was picked by Leroy Gilmore who didn't like it and traded it for a model airplane that some other kid got. I picked a comb I didn't like, and no one would trade with me.

During the party, my classmates talked about the bicycles, trains, dolls, and toys they expected to get for Christmas. When the party was over, the teacher asked me to stay a few minutes. When we were alone, she asked if I wanted to take home the classroom's Christmas tree.

"Sure!" I said with tears of joy in my eyes. It was a miracle! *A miracle* I thought as I rushed home with it. Wait until Mama sees it.

It was only two feet tall, and it didn't win any prizes, but to me it was the most beautiful Christmas tree in the world.

When I brought it home, everyone was excited.

Ma did her cross and blessed it.

We all argued about where we should put it. We finally decided to put it on a small table in the corner of the kitchen, next to the window.

The neighbors came by the dozens to examine it. Some admired it, others thought it was ugly.

We added more decorations to it. Small trinkets, beads, pieces of glass, anything that shined or glistened.

When Papa came home and saw the tree, we all held our breath. He broke out into a broad smile and said, "What a **beautiful** tree!"

"*O Yianaki mas* brought it home from school," Mama proudly explained.

40

"Bravo Yianaki!" My father hugged me.

On Christmas eve we hung our stockings around the tree and lay awake all night listening for the sounds of hooves on the roof which was three stories above us.

When we awoke the next morning, we rushed into the kitchen and found that Santa Claus had been there. Our stockings were filled with chestnuts, tangerines, and koulourakia. And under the tree was a harmonica for me, wrapped in beautiful Christmas paper.

It was the happiest Christmas I ever had.

Kalla Christouyina! (Merry Christmas!)

The National Anthem

I couldn't speak a word of English when I started kindergarten. However, all that changed by the time I reached the fourth grade.

One day, Miss Barrett was teaching us about the flags of different countries. She pointed to the large American flag she brought in to our classroom from the auditorium and asked, "Who can tell me how many stars and stripes the American flag contains?"

Mary Robinson was the first to raise her hand.

Miss Barrett smiled, "Yes, Mary?"

Mary Robinson stood up, "Our flag has forty eight stars, one for each state in the union and thirteen stripes, one for each of the thirteen colonies."

Mary Robinson was the smartest girl in our class. She spoke perfect English, knew how to spell practically every word in the dictionary, and I hated her.

"Very good, Mary," Miss Barrett said, and then she showed us a large chart filled with color sketches of flags from other countries.

"If you look at this chart, you will see that each country has its own flag."

My hand immediately shot up when I recognized the Greek flag on the chart.

"I see the Greek flag! It's that one. The one with the blue stripes and white cross."

Miss Barrett checked the chart and smiled, "Very good, Johnnie."

I smiled back, proud that I knew something Mary Robinson didn't know. I focused my attention again on what Miss Barrett was saying.

"In addition to having its own flag, each country also has its own national anthem. Who can tell me what our national anthem is? Mary."

"The name of our national anthem is *The Star Spangled Banner*."

My hand shot up before Miss Barrett could say, "Thank you, Mary."

"Yes, Johnnie?"

"I know the Greek national anthem," I said proudly.

"You do?" Miss Barrett was quite impressed.

"Yes 'mam."

"Can you sing it for us?"

"Sure I can" I said as I strutted to the front of the class.

"Class! Please stand at attention and put your right hand over your heart. Johnnie Kallas is going to sing us the Greek national anthem."

"Go ahead, Johnnie." Miss Barrett said, as she stood at attention with the rest of the class. Her right hand was placed over her heart and her eyes were closed. Mary Robinson was annoyed over the fuss Miss Barrett was making over this.

I was in my glory when I belted out the first line of the Greek National Anthem. *"Se ynorizo apo tin kopsi tou spathiou"* (pause) Oh...oh. It suddenly occurred to me, that I only knew the first line. I glanced at Miss Barrett. She still had her eyes closed, expecting to hear the entire anthem.

The Greek kids in the back of the room were no help. They knew I was in trouble and so did I, so I faked it! I stuck with the tune and made up my own Greek words.

Vegetables: *"me maroulia, kai kremithia, me fasolia, kai angouia. "* I soon ran out of vegetables. I looked up and Miss Barrett still had her eyes closed, so I continued with the clothes I was wearing, *"Me pokamiso, kai papoutsia, me skaltses, kai kravanta, "* and finally finished on a high note *"Kai na mei xehasete ta sovraka mou "*...(my underwear.)

When Miss Barrett opened her eyes, they were filled with tears. "Oh Johnnie, that was so beautiful. Thank you. Thank you, so much."

She had the class applaud as I walked back to my seat. The Greek kids giggled and Mary Robinson stuck out her tongue at me.

I loved going to school.

Spelling Bee

If I ever become president, the first thing I would do is outlaw spelling bees. I would pass a law that any teacher caught giving a spelling bee in her class would be expelled from school and sentenced to life in prison.

These were the thoughts running through my mind as Mary Robinson and Leroy Gilmore strutted to the opposite sides of the classroom and started to choose their teams for the spelling bee, a ritual that occurred each morning in our fourth grade class at Robert Treat School in Newark, New Jersey.

Mary Robinson called out, "Mildred Grossman." She always picked Mildred Grossman first. Next to Mary Robinson and Leroy Gilmore, she was the best speller in our class. And so it went, back and forth, Mary Robinson and Leroy Gilmore carefully selecting the members of their spelling bee teams. First all the good spellers were chosen, then the average spellers, until only the poor spellers were left wondering which team would get stuck with them. This process seemed to take forever. Finally, I was the only one left to be chosen.

Leroy Gilmore scowled as he muttered, "John Kallas."

My teammates greeted me with disgust as I took my place at the end of the line. Mary Robinson was all smiles.

Miss Barrett, our teacher, called out the first word to be spelled: "**Redeem**."

"**Redeem**," Mary Robinson continued to smile, as she quickly spelled "**r..e..d..e..e..m**."

I knew how to spell that word. Back and forth it went. So far, I knew how to spell every word the teacher had called out. So did the other kids. As my turn rapidly approached, I prayed, "Please God, give me a word that I can spell. Please don't let me be the first to sit down. Oh..oh, here it comes."

"**Foreign**."

"**Foreign**," I said, clearing my throat "**f..o..r..**" (So far, so good. Now, is it **e..i..g..n** or **i..e..g..n**?)

Everyone's attention was focused on me as I tried to remember the rule: (i comes before e, except after c ..or was it.. e comes before i except after c?) Miss Barrett was losing her patience.

"John?" Miss Barrett whispered, slightly irritated.

"Foreign," I said again "F..o..r..i..e..g..n..?"

"No, John, it's **f..o..r..e..i..g..n.** You may sit down."

Mary Robinson and and her team roared with delight, and my team groaned with despair while I walked back to my desk and sat in my chair. And there I sat for what seemed like hours before another word was misspelled.

After all these years, I have finally learned to spell correctly. I now use *Spell Check* on my word processor.

Somebody's Going to Die

During the Depression, my mother worked the nine to midnight shift at Clark's Thread Company. So each morning, the four of us kids would awaken ourselves, get dressed, make breakfast, and go to school while Mama slept with the covers drawn over her head.

One morning she awoke just as we were going out the door.

"Stop!" She screamed out from her bedroom. We stopped in dead in our tracks.

"What Mama?"

She stuck her head out from under the covers and in a trembling voice filled with terror she cried out, "I dreamt that a white bird flew into our house!"

"A white bird?"

"Oh, oh. That means somebody's going to die."

"It also means no school for us today."

My mother ordered us back to bed and stuck her head back under the covers. She believed that death was hovering over us, so we stayed home from school as a safety precaution.

Staying home was great, until our friends came home from school.

"Mama! Can we go out and play?"

"Are you crazy?" She reminded us of her dream.

"Aw Mama!"

This meant that we were not allowed to leave the safety of our home until someone out there died. This could take days or even weeks, which it once did. So all we could do was wait.

This time we only had to wait three days. That's when the mailman told us that his ninety-two year old grandmother in Alabama passed away. My mother did her cross and told us to go out and play.

The next morning, we each took a note to school that I wrote in English and my mother signed in Greek.

My teacher read the note:

Dear Teacher,

Please forgive my son, John Kallas, for being absent for the past three days. I dreamt a white bird flew into our house, so I had to keep him home.

Yours truly,
Ahlayia Kaloyerinis

She looked up and asked, "A white bird?"

"Yes 'mam. It means that somebody's going to die."

"And the three days?" She was still puzzled.

"That's how long it took before we found out that the mailman's ninety-two-year-old grandmother in Alabama had passed away."

My teacher closed her eyes and told me to take my seat.

I couldn't understand why she was so upset. So, I didn't say anything and took my seat.

47

Growing Up to be an Engineer

I have been told that when I was born, my father held me in his arms and immediately announced to the world that he had a son who would someday become a great engineer. Thus, within the first few moments of life, my destiny was set.

So from the day I was born it was always my job to repair anything that broke or needed fixing in our house. This included clotheslines that got stuck in the rope pulleys, toasters, door bells, broken windows, and radio tubes and blown fuses that had to be replaced.

My father beamed with pride, when I built a crystal radio that worked with a cat's whisker, a crystal, and wire wrapped around an oatmeal box, or when I built a model airplane that flew with a twisted rubber band.

In elementary school, I excelled in arithmetic, science and drawing. However, I did poorly in reading and writing because of my difficulty with English.

During this time Papa worked as a counterman at the London Lunch, which was located close to the Newark College of Engineering. Engineering students would give him arithmetic problems to bring home for me to solve.

If it takes three minutes for a one-inch water faucet to fill a ten-gallon bucket, how long would it take for a two-inch water faucet to fill a five-gallon bucket?

If Johnny can paint a fence in three hours and Tommy can do it in two hours, how long would it take for the two of them to paint the fence together?

Luckily, I had a sympathetic arithmetic teacher who would stay with me after class and translate these problems into numbers that I could add, subtract, divide, and multiply. She made it all look so easy. I would then give the answers to Papa, who would check them with the engineering students.

Everybody was happy. My teacher enjoyed helping me, Papa was proud of my ability to solve these complex problems, and the engineering students got an extra bowl of soup on the house.

Doing My Homework with Papa

In 1927, I brought home my first homework. I was in the first grade where we were learning to read and write. My father quietly stood behind me and watched me as I copied the letters as they were shown in my first grade writing book. Fascinated with what I was doing, he picked up my book and carefully examined it.

"They let you take this book home?" he asked.

"Yes Papa. We have to bring our books home to do our homework."

"Homework? *Ti pai na pi* (what is) *homework?*"

"It's school work we have to do at home each night."

Papa pulled up a chair and sat next to me. "That's fantastic! You must teach me everything you learn in class. And each night, we will do the homework together!"

"Sure Papa. It's real easy!"

"Good! Let's begin now. What did you learn in class today?"

"We're learning the alphabet... This is the way we write the letter A'."

My father watched me write the letter A and quickly wrote it himself.

"Hah! Hah! That was easy! A! It's the same as the Greek letter, *alpha.* "

"Good Papa, now let's write the letter B."

My father had difficulty in pronouncing the letter B. "We don't have the letter 'B' in Greek. Look! They write it like our *veta!* "

"Good, now write the letter C ... C ... A, B, C!"

"C .. Another letter we don't have. C .. A .. B .. C! How am I doing, *Yianni?*"

"Very good, Papa!"

"A .. B .. C! *Bravo Yiannaki!* You are a good teacher!"

Papa put on his jacket and cap. Holding his homework paper high over his head, he shouted with joy, "A .. B .. C! I am going to the *kafeneo* to show my friends how I can now write in English!"

And so it went. For years, every night after supper I would have to teach Papa what I learned in school that day, which included math, science, and Social Studies. I had to make sure I understood everything that was taught in class because I knew Papa would be asking me questions on anything he didn't understand. After teaching him what I had learned in class, we would both do the homework.

One day Miss Gieger, my sixth grade Social Studies teacher asked us to cut out an article from a newspaper and bring it to class where we would read and discuss it.

Papa became quite excited about this assignment. "We must choose an article that has great social significance!" He said as he frantically searched through a half dozen back issues of *The Daily Worker*.

"Aw, Papa!"

"Ahah! Here it is! *Karl Marx's theory on 'surplus value'!*"

My father carefully cut out the article and had me read it a dozen times until I read it perfectly. He then spent hours explaining what it meant. Finally satisfied that I thoroughly understood the importance of this theory, he let me go to bed.

"You must be well rested when you discuss your article in class tomorrow."

"Yeah, sure. (yawn) Good night, Papa."

The next morning, I was the first to raise my hand when Miss Gieger asked who was ready to read and discuss their article.

I stood before the class and slowly read my article with great care and precision. Out of the corner of my eye, I detected my teacher's discomfort every time I mentioned *"Lenin"* or the *"People's Revolution"*.

Halfway through the article, she stopped me.

"John, where in heaven's name did you find that article?"

"*The Daily Worker*. Why?"

"Oh dear, oh dear, dear." She was upset.

"You told us to cut an article out of a newspaper. You didn't say which one."

"Well, I'm sorry but we're not allowed to read anything from *that* paper."

"Why not?"

"See me after class.   Now, please sit down."

The class giggled as I sat down.

That night, when Papa came home from work, he was anxious to find out how well we did in Social Studies.

"Did the teacher like our article?"

"Papa, she wouldn't let me read it in class."

"What? Why not?"

"I don't know why, Papa.   She wants me to write a 300-word essay on *Why the United States is the best country in the world* and read it to the class."

Papa was obviously stunned by what had happened in school but after a few moments, he quickly recovered.

"Ah good! Good!" he exclaimed, "I will help you write it!"

"Aw, Papa."

Why? It's Not Saturday!

All through the prohibition years Papa made his own beer, wine, and whiskey. No, Papa was not breaking the law. The law was quite simple: *You could make it, if you didn't sell it.*

Each year he would fill a huge wooden barrel next to the kitchen stove with water, sugar, yeast, and the grape skins left over from his wine making.

Papa covered the barrel with an old wooden board and told us, "In three weeks, these grape skins will have fermented enough to be distilled into pure alcohol."

This meant that in three weeks we were scheduled to get the 15-gallon still with all its accessories. I didn't know who owned this still. All I knew was that we got it each year from the Lavakos family and five days later, when we were finished with it, we would deliver it to the Trafalis family.

That night while we slept the fermentation began. *Gurgle, gurgle, glug, gurgle, gurgle, swusssh!* Each day Mama added orange peels, spoiled tangerines, and anything else that would ferment. *Gurgle, gurgle, glug, gurgle, gurgle, swusssh!* The fermentation continued day and night.

At the end of the third week, I came home from school and found the 15-gallon copper tank and its accessories piled on the kitchen floor. I didn't waste any time assembling everything in our bathroom.

First, I put the two wooden boards across the bathtub. On one board I placed the cooling tank and hooked it up to the water faucet; on the other board, I connected the small gas stove to the gas jet sticking out of our bathroom wall. Finally, I set the empty copper tank on the gas stove. Everything that was needed to do this came with the still including a small wrench and a pair of pliers.

When Papa came home from work, he checked my connections and filled the still with the fermenting grape skins. He then lit the small gas range that the still was set on. Within a half hour, alcohol started to drip out of the condensation coil and into an empty milk bottle. *Drip! Drip! Drip!*

The alcohol had no color and looked like water; however, it smelled and tasted terrible. Papa explained that the alcohol would have to be distilled again at least two or three times before it became pure.

Papa showed us how to check the alcoholic content by spilling a few drops on the enamel kitchen table and lighting it with a match.

My sister, Helen, and I took turns all night watching the still while Papa slept. I was nine and my sister was eight at that time. My two brothers were too young to be given such a responsibility.

Each time a milk bottle became full, we would replace it with an empty one and check its alcohol content. If the still became clogged and started to shake and rumble, we would turn off the gas and wake up Papa to unclog it.

The most boring job we had was flushing the used distilled grape skins down the toilet. It seemed to take hours for the toilet tank to refill after each flush. Needless to say, our hair and bodies became saturated with the stench of fermented grape skins and distilled liquor.

Mercifully, the entire operation was suspended when Papa went to work in the morning. We went to school afterwards as if nothing had happened the night before.

I had a tough time staying awake in my class. Mrs. Davis was teaching us about Florida.

"The Everglades are located in . . ," She stopped in the middle of her sentence and sniffed. *Sniff! Sniff!* She continued walking up and down each aisle, stopping at each student's desk and sniffing as she talked. "Many alligators live in the Everglades." *Sniff! Sniff!*

Soon the whole class was sniffing. I couldn't smell a thing. Mrs. Davis finally stopped sniffing when she reached my desk.

"John, please come out into the hallway with me," she said as she gently escorted me out of the classroom. When we were in the hallway she told me to go home immediately and take a bath.

"Why?" I said, "It's not Saturday!"

"Go! Go!" she cried out and returned to the classroom leaving me standing in the hallway totally dumbfounded. For years we all took a bath once a week on Saturdays, and no one ever complained.

As I left the school and headed home, I saw my sister also leaving the school. She was in tears because her teacher told her to go home and take a bath. When we got home Mama, who had worked the night shift at Clark's Thread Company, was still sleeping with the covers pulled over her head.

"Ma!" we called out to her.

She mumbled something from under the covers and went back to sleep.

"Ma!" we shouted, "our teachers said we have to take a bath immediately!"

She stuck her head out from under the covers and with a stunned look cried out, "Why? It's not Saturday!"

As it turned out, it was Wednesday, so we stayed home the rest of the week and took our bath on Saturday, after we disassembled the still and delivered it to the Trafalis family.

The Library Card

Our parents who were Greek, never brought home any periodicals or books written in English. They couldn't read them, and even if they could, they were too expensive to buy, so the only access we had to these materials was to borrow them from the public library.

Newark, New Jersey had one of the finest public library systems in the country. Each neighborhood had a small library filled with wonderful books for children of all ages. Ours was located on Norfolk Street, just a few blocks from West Market Street where all the Greeks lived.

The main library was a huge, six-story stone building located downtown on Washington Street. It had long, marble stairs and huge columns and was filled with practically every book ever written.

I had borrowed and read practically every book they had in the neighborhood library, so I was very upset when they told me that I had to graduate from elementary school before I could get a card to the main library.

The day I graduated from elementary school I rushed to my neighborhood library, showed them my diploma, and applied for a card to the main library. They were expecting me and had my card ready. I couldn't believe my eyes when I saw my name stamped on the metal tab attached to the card.

With my new card clutched in my hand I ran downtown to the main library and rushed up those marble stairs. I tripped and fell face down on the stairs. Out of breath and with my nose bleeding, I finally entered the main library. A librarian was standing close by and greeted me.

"Shhh!" she whispered. "What do you want?"

Still panting and wiping the blood from my nose, I showed her my brand new library card.

"Mam," I said. "I want the biggest book you have in this library."

She smiled and whispered, "Follow me, young man."

Wow! I thought. It was the first time I was called a young man. Hah! Why not? I have a card to the main library, don't I?

I couldn't believe it. *We took an elevator to the third floor.* That's how big this library was. After we got off the elevator I followed the librarian through miles of library stacks filled with a million books. She finally stopped and reached up and handed me this huge book.

"Here, is *The Count of Monte Cristo* by Alexander Dumas." she whispered. "It was the first big book I read, when I got my card to the main library."

Chapter Five

The Teenage Years

My Byzantium Plan

Growing up as Greek-Americans and dealing with the two cultures became more difficult as we grew older. It was especially difficult for someone like my younger sister, Helen, a beautiful teenager who liked boys and loved to dance. She was not allowed to go to the movies or attend any social affair without her family or older brother.

Helen and I worked out a system whereby I would take her to the movies on Saturday nights. When we got downtown, she would take off with her date and I would go to the movies by myself. After the movie, we would meet under the Bamberger Clock and come home together.

A major problem erupted when my father told Helen she could not go to the High School Junior Prom unless I took her.

"But Papa, I can't go to the prom with my brother!" She cried.

"Then don't go. *Teliose to zitaima* (End of discussion)."

Poor Helen. Not going to the prom was the worst thing that could possibly happen to her. With tears in her eyes, she turned to me for help.

"Talk to him, Johnnie. He'll listen to you."

"Don't worry, " I told her. "I'll figure out something."

I had a Byzantium plan in mind. I was sure that Papa would let Helen go to the prom with my best friend, Johnny Johnson, whose Greek name was *Yianni Yianniou*. After all, he was like a member of the family; he was Greek and Papa trusted him.

The following day when I saw Johnny at school, I put my plan into action.

"Johnny, I need your help."

"Forget it. I'm not taking your sister to the prom."

"How did you know?"

"I know everything that goes on in your family."

"I thought you were my friend?"

"I am and what you're trying to do won't work. Besides, I hate dancing."

"You don't have to dance. Just take her there and bring her back."

"I said, 'No.'"

"I'll pay you ten dollars."

"Ten dollars? Where the hell are you going to get that kind of money?"

"I have it right here" I said, showing him a brand new ten dollar bill.

"First, you have to ask her."

"Supposing she refuses?"

"You keep the ten."

"Supposing your father says no?"

"You still keep the ten."

"Hmm? (pause) It's a deal."

"There's one condition."

"What's that?"

"This must be kept secret."

"You can trust me."

"If Helen finds out that I paid you to take her to the prom, she will kill me."

"I said, You can trust me."

I handed Johnny the ten dollar bill. He carefully examined both sides of it before he slipped it into his pocket.

"When are you going to ask her?"

"This afternoon."

"Good. The sooner, the better."

I had to work after school that day. I worked at the Paramount Theatre as an usher so I didn't get home until very late. The minute I walked in, I knew my plan had worked. Helen was waiting up for me, all smiles.

"Johnnie! You will never guess what happened! Johnny Johnson asked me to the prom and Papa said I could go!"

"Great!"

My Byzantium plan worked! I never saw my sister so happy.

59

The Sons of Pericles

When I was a teenager, I belonged to The Sons of Pericles as did all Greek teenage boys in Newark.

Belonging to The Sons of Pericles meant playing basketball, which was great. I enjoyed playing basketball with my Greek buddies, especially when we played against the black kids in Newark. It was a real challenge since they were two to five feet taller than us. It wasn't that we Greeks were short. They were just tall, that's all.

Despite this disadvantage, we managed to beat them every time. How? We would simply call the signals to each other in Greek.

Pano, Paneyoti, Pano! meant High, Peter, throw the ball high.

I remember this one big game we were playing. I was dribbling the ball down the court, when I heard, *Piso Yianni, Piso!*

Without hesitation, I threw the ball behind me. I then turned, saw this big black kid smiling with the basketball in his hands.

"Piso Yianni, Piso!" he laughs, "I done broke their code!"

Yes, The Sons of Pericles lost that night.

The Maids of Athens

All of the Greek teenage boys in Newark belonged to the Sons of Pericles and their teenage sisters belonged to the Maids of Athens.

The big event of the year for the Greeks in Newark was the basketball game and dance sponsored by the Maids of Athens. Naturally the Greeks were thrilled to see the Sons of Pericles play the basketball game that preceded the dance with such speed, skill, and agility.

Our parents and relatives would yell, "*Bravo Palikaria!* " every time we made a basket. With our parents in the stands, we played extra hard and never lost a game.

After the game, we would shower, get dressed, and attend the dance that was being held on the gym floor. My friends were already on the dance floor while our parents sat or stood along the side walls proudly watching us dance.

I was dancing with Kiki Alevras when, out of the corner of my eye, I noticed Kiki's mother move next to my mother. Both of them had that gleam in their eyes as we swept past them dancing the *Peabody* with incredible charm and grace.

I could only imagine what they were saying to each other in Greek.

"Ach! They make such a fine couple."

"Kiki has grown into such a beautiful woman."

"And your son, *Yianni*, is no longer a small boy. He has grown into a handsome young man."

"Yes. And he's very smart, too. He's going to be an engineer."

"Ach, wouldn't it be wonderful if ..."

"Yes, it certainly would."

They crossed themselves and prayed, *Please, God, let it happen.*

They were praying that Kiki and I would become romantically involved, get married, and have five or six children.

It was true, Kiki was very beautiful and charming. But we grew up together like brother and sister. And it is not possible to have romantic thoughts about someone who is like your sister. Besides, she was Peter Alevras' sister, who happened to be my best friend.

After we finished dancing, I asked Mary Poulos, the best dancer in the Maids of Athens, to dance with me. As we danced the *Double Lindy*, out of the corner of my eye I could see Mary's mother standing next to my mother. Both were watching us with that gleam in their eyes.

After awhile the Greek music started. We all joined hands, young and old, and danced to the Greek folk songs. It was a real joy to watch Papa lead the line, jump high in the air, and slap the back of his heel in time with the music. Much to my surprise, even Mama joined the line of dancers.

"Yasoo! Manula mou!" I proudly called out to her.

Although there were no romantic feelings exchanged that night, there was enough real love on that dance floor to last us a lifetime.

Thank you, my beautiful Maids of Athens. Thank you forever.

No Room For Secrets

When I was sixteen, we went on our first vacation. We rented a small cottage in Maine for two weeks. It was there that I met and fell in love with Vickie Cassavant, a beautiful blond fifteen year-old girl from Montreal, Canada.

On our last day, we exchanged addresses and promised to write to each other. I also managed to summon enough courage to kiss her goodbye on the cheek.

When we returned to Newark, I was like a lovesick puppy. I was the first to write to her. I rewrote that letter at least fifteen times before I was satisfied with the handwriting and that there were no misspelled words.

In the letter I told her that I had just come back from horseback riding, which wasn't a complete fabrication since I did go horseback riding once a long time ago.

Anyway I mailed the letter and each day after that I would anxiously check the mail for her response.

One night I came home late from my job as an usher and found my family sitting in the kitchen. My brothers and sister were grinning from ear to ear.

My sister was the first to say something. "Does your behind still hurt from horseback riding?"

Oh my God, I thought. I must have written the wrong address on my letter to Vickie and it was returned.

"What are you talking about?" I asked.

"Your girlfriend, Vickie, answered your letter and we all read it," she said as she handed me a letter that was ripped open.

"You read my mail?" I was furious.

She ran behind Papa, who was sitting at the table reading his newspaper.

"Papa said it was alright for us to read it."

"Papa, did you tell Helen, it was alright to read my mail?"

"Yes I did. Why?"

"Because it's not right for her to do that, Papa."

"Why not?"

"*Ti pai na pi* personal?" he asked.

"It means that there may be something in there that I don't want her to know about!"

Papa put down his newspaper, looked me straight in the eye and asked, "What could possibly be in that letter that you wouldn't want your sister or anyone else in the family to know about?"

I couldn't answer him, because we were raised to share everything. There was never any room for any secrets in our family.

Chapter Six
World War II

Dog Tags

When America entered World War II, I joined the Army and immediately went to Fort Dix, New Jersey to be processed. The first thing they did when I arrived was to stamp out a pair of dog tags, which I would wear around my neck until I was discharged. Stamped on these metal dog tags were your name, rank, serial number, blood type, and religion.

However, Army regulations prevented me from having "G.O." (Greek Orthodox) stamped on my dog tags. I had to have a "P" (Protestant), "C" (Catholic), or "H" (Hebrew) stamped on my dog tags. I argued with them. I told them that Greek Orthodox was the only true religion.

"If you don't believe me," I said, "ask any Greek. He'll tell you!"

But, they didn't listen to me. Apparently, the army has finally seen the light. Greek-Americans serving in the military can now have "G.O." stamped on their dog tags. They also have Greek Orthodox priests serve as chaplains.

Amen.

Papa's Pictures

When we were children we were always drawing pictures. It was something we learned from Papa, who was quite an artist. Every time he sat at the kitchen table to draw, we would gather around him and watch his every move.

He loved to draw pictures of the different Greek battleships, all flying the Greek flag. He drew them all from memory, and the only drawing tool he used was an ordinary pencil.

The picture he enjoyed drawing the most was the destroyer he served on when he was in the Greek Navy during World War I. Each detail was drawn with incredible accuracy and loving care.

And with each picture, Papa had an exciting story to tell. The walls of our bedroom and kitchen were filled with his pictures.

In elementary school I was always drawing pictures. In high school I majored in drafting and drew cartoons for our high school yearbook. When I graduated, I was chosen *class artist* by my classmates.

In the Army I was never without my sketch pad. I continuously drew sketches of my buddies and cartoons for the camp newspaper.

In 1943 when I boarded a troop ship to go overseas, I had my duffel bag slung over my shoulder and a sketch pad under my arm.

Our troop ship was a small liberty ship, making its maiden voyage. The quarters assigned to my company were in "G" deck, the bottom deck towards the back of the ship next to the propeller shaft.

The constant grinding noise of the shaft and the smell of vomit made it impossible to sleep in these quarters, so I took my sketch pad, some pencils, and went up on deck for the rest of my voyage across the Atlantic.

Bam! There were two destroyers constantly circling our ship using a catapult device to fling garbage cans filled with explosives into the air behind them. When the cans hit the water, they would sink and after a few seconds, they would explode. Bam! This was done to keep the German submarines away from us.

Bam! Every two minutes the cans would fly into the air. When one destroyer ran out of explosives, another destroyer loaded with a fresh supply would take its place. Bam!

After sketching the destroyers from every possible angle, I became fascinated with the radar antenna spinning at the top of our ship. I climbed to the upper deck so I could draw it in greater detail. My four years of high school drafting came in very handy as I drew the antenna assembly in perfect proportion. I included every nut and bolt.

Boy, wait until Papa sees these sketches I thought.

That's when two towering marine guards approached me and arrested me for being a spy.

"What? Me, a spy?" I yelled, "Are you crazy?"

One marine handcuffed me and the other gathered my sketches and sketch pad as *evidence.*

As I was being hauled into the brig, I called out to one of my buddies, "Get Starr! Get Captain Starr!"

When we got to the brig, a marine lieutenant started to grill me.

"What's your name, Corporal?"

"John Kallas, sir!"

I tried to salute, but I couldn't with my hands handcuffed.

The lieutenant nodded to the marine that cuffed me, "Take off the cuffs."

The lieutenant carefully examined each of my sketches. He seemed particularly interested in my sketches of the radar antenna.

"Where did you learn to draw like this, Corporal?"

"My father, sir. He was in the Greek Navy during World War I, sir. And when we were kids, he would always draw pictures of Greek battleships and destroyers."

"Why did you pick this particular radar antenna to draw? You drew it in such precise proportion. You drew every detail, every nut and bolt."

"I took four years of drafting in Central High School in Newark, sir."

"You didn't answer my question, Corporal."

"Sorry sir. What was the question?"

"Why did you pick this particular radar antenna to draw?"

"I don't know why. It was there, so I drew it."

"Did you know the design of this antenna is top *top* secret?"

"No sir, I didn't." I was stunned.

"What the hell is going on here?" A voice bellows out.

Thank God, It was my Captain.

"Now, what did you do, Kallas?"

"Nothing sir. I was just drawing some pictures."

"Captain, your corporal is a spy."

"What? Kallas a spy? You gotta' be kidding!"

"Look at the drawings he made of our top secret radar antenna. Pay particular attention to the precise detail he drew of every nut and bolt. Captain, only a trained German spy could..."

"Captain, I tried to tell him about my father being in the Greek Navy and how..."

"Quiet, Kallas. Let me handle this."

The captain turns to the lieutenant, "Lieutenant, I know this man and he is no spy. He's always drawing pictures and talking about his Greek father. Release him and I will take personal responsibility for his behavior."

"He won't draw any more pictures while aboard this ship?"

"I guarantee it."

"Okay. Then he can go."

Relieved, I reached for my sketch pad, "Can I have my sketch pad, sir?"

"Get him out of here before I change my mind."

I knew then that I would have to wait until after the war to draw that radar antenna from memory, the way Papa drew his Greek battleships.

When Greek Meets Greek

Anyone growing up as a Greek-American has been asked at one time or another What happens when one Greek meets another Greek?

Well, I would like to tell you a story about what happened when this Greek met another Greek.

During World War II, the First Allied Airborne Army, which included my battalion, suffered enormous casualties during the jump into Normandy and Holland. So, in early August we returned to our barracks in England to await replacements.

I was lying in my bunk reading a Yank magazine, when a flood of new replacements rushed into our barracks to claim the empty bunks for themselves. A tall, lanky soldier with thick black hair, a moustache, and a long hawk-like nose, stopped at my bunk and pointed to the empty bunk below me and asked, "Is this bunk taken?"

"Nope!"

This guy looks like a genuine Turk, I thought as I watched him drop his heavy duffel bag and unpack.

"What's your name, soldier?" I asked.

He stood up and raised his fists, "*Venezelos Psomiades!* Wanna' make something out of it?"

"Hah! Hah!", I burst out laughing, "No, you ugly Greek!"

He put down his fists and asked, "How did you know I was Greek?"

"It takes one to know one! Where you from?"

"Saco, Maine."

"Saco, Maine? You have to be kidding!"

"Why?"

"I was born in Saco, Maine."

"Can't be! I know every Greek family in Saco."

"My family moved to Newark when I was a baby."

70

Needless to say, we instantly became buddies and looked out for each other during the Battle of the Bulge, the jump across the Rhine, and the push through the Ruhr Valley. We witnessed the horror of Dachau and were together when we finally hooked up with the Russians.

Van was my best man when I married Ginette and also godfather to my son Jean Louis.

No, we never opened a restaurant.

The Roosevelt Letters

It was early April, 1945 when it happened. My company, along with the rest of the 18th Airborne Corps, was headed for the Ruhr pocket deep inside Germany. We had just crossed the Elbe River and were disembarking when I noticed something odd happening on the other side of the river. There was a long line of Patton's tanks parked alongside the road with all of the tankers sitting on their tanks reading the Army newspaper, *Stars and Stripes*. An entire battalion of infantry soldiers was on the other side of the road, sitting on their helmets reading *Stars and Stripes*.

Why is everyone reading *Stars and Stripes* I wondered. That's when I saw the two-word headline that filled the entire front page. "FDR DEAD!"

"What happened?" I called out to the soldiers reading the paper.

"Dunno!"

"Just sez he's dead!"

We were stunned as we climbed into the two-ton trucks waiting for us.

"Roosevelt dead?"

"Hard to believe."

"Hey! We all hafta' go sooner or later!"

"Yeah, but not Roosevelt!"

"Why couldn't it have been Hitler instead?"

"Who the hell knows?"

I kept thinking about poor Papa. Papa must be devastated by this I thought. He really loved Roosevelt.

Whenever Roosevelt gave a fireside chat, all of us would sit around the old Philco radio and listen to every word. To this day, I can hear him saying, "The only thing we have to fear is fear itself!"

In one of his fireside chats Roosevelt asked us to support his National Recovery Administration (NRA). Papa immediately instructed us not to buy anything if it did not have the blue NRA seal. Papa argued, "We have to let him know that he has our support."

"We can write him a letter," my sister, Helen, said.

"You can do that!"

"We did in class last week. We all wrote the president a letter and sent it to him."

"Where did you send it?"

"The White House, where he lives."

"Bravo, *Elenaki mou!*"

My sister beamed with pride.

My father then turned his attention to me, "*Yianni*, we must also write him a letter. Go get a pen and paper."

"Aw Papa. Do we have to?"

"Do as your father says, quickly!" Mama spoke out.

So I reluctantly gave Papa my Parker fountain pen and a piece of notebook paper. "Here you are, Papa."

"No. No. You write. I will tell you what to say."

"Okay Papa, I'm ready."

"Dear Mr. President Roosevelt. (pause) I hear your speech on radio tonight, and I ..."

"Not so fast, Papa." I was writing as fast as I could. I was eleven years old at the time and still had difficulty with my spelling and penmanship. After a few minutes, I was ready again, "Okay, Go ahead."

"My name is Louis Kallas and your speech tonight gave us great hope. *Thelo na sou rotiso yia to NRA...*"

"Aw Papa!"

My mother urged me to continue writing. "*Grapse! Grapse!*"

It wasn't easy translating Papa's peasant Greek into my poor English; however, I finally finished the letter. Papa carefully signed it with great pride and reverence. I addressed the envelope, put a three-cent stamp on it, and mailed it that same night.

Much to my surprise, we received a reply from the White House on the following Tuesday. When Papa came home from work, we immediately handed him the letter.

"It's from the White House, Papa."

"President Roosevelt?"

"Did you open it?"

"No Papa. It's addressed to you."

Papa was stunned as he examined the thick envelope.

"The President of the United States answered my letter."

"Aren't you going to open it?"

My father carefully slit open the envelope with his pocket knife and took out the letter.

"What does he say?"

"Read it, Papa."

He handed me the letter, "*Na. thiavisto esie.* (Here, you read it.) I want to listen."

"Dear Mr. Kallas…"

Papa put his arm around my shoulder, "He knows our name! The President of the United States knows our name."

"Wow!"

I continued to read, "I received your letter today and I sincerely thank you for your interest in the *New Deal.* Democracy can only survive through the active support of its citizens."

Papa nodded in agreement, "True, true."

"I have enclosed the information you asked for pertaining to the National Recovery Administration (NRA). If you have any other questions, please do not hesitate to write to me. Sincerely yours, Franklin Delano Roosevelt, President of the United States."

"Look, Papa, he even signed it. "

Papa examined the letter again.

"Franklin Delano Roosevelt, President of the United States. Hah! Wait until I show them this letter at work."

I pulled out a bundle of pamphlets and literature from the envelope.

"Look at all the extra stuff he sent us, Papa."

"Good! After supper we will read and study all of it!"

"But Papa, there's so much."

Papa continued, "And then we will write another letter."

"Aw Papa."

After that letter, writing to Roosevelt on Tuesday nights became a regular weekly routine.

Rat! Tat! Tat! The sound of machine gun fire suddenly erupted!

Messerschmidts!

Our truck swerved to the side of the road and came to a screeching stop.

We jumped out of our trucks, dove for cover, and hugged the ground for dear life as two Messerschmidt fighter planes strafed our convoy.

BAM! Bam! Bam! The earth shuddered as their bullets ripped into the ground.

Roosevelt is dead. I felt a fright that I never, felt before.

Chapter Seven

After The War

Papa's Olive Oil

When Ginette, my French warbride, and Jean-Louis, my six-month old son, came to the States after World War II, there was an acute shortage of housing. So, we lived with Mom and Papa on Avon Avenue in Newark. It wasn't bad. Ginette spoke French to Mom, and Mom spoke Greek to Ginette. They communicated beautifully.

Papa had a ball with his first grandchild. He enjoyed picking him up, hugging him, and smothering him with kisses. However, when the thought crossed his mind that Jean-Louis was baptized a Catholic, he would drop him as if he was a rotten fish.

"Ach!" he would cry, "Why didn't you baptize him in a Greek Orthodox church?"

"Papa, he was born in a small town in France that didn't have a Greek church. Besides, what the hell difference does it make?"

"It makes a big difference," he would say.

He was right. There is a big difference. I've seen Catholic priests baptize a half dozen babies in less than three minutes by saying a few Latin words and dabbing a little oil on each baby's forehead.

Baptizing a baby in a Greek Orthodox church is a major operation that can last hours. First, the baby's clothes are removed. Then, the baby's naked body is covered from head to toe with olive oil. Finally, the priest holds the oil-soaked baby high over his head, chants an ancient ritual, and then plunges the baby into a brass tub filled with water. The priest holds the terrified baby's head under water while he chants some more.

"Yes Papa, there is a difference and I'm sorry. But what's done is done."

There was no doubt about how precious Jean-Louis was to Papa. His next most precious possession was his olive oil. Once a month I would go to Hoboken, board some Greek ship docked there, and pick up a five-gallon tin can of olive oil sent to us by our family in Greece.

Papa would always tell us, "This oil was squeezed from olives that came from trees that have belonged to our family for thousands of years."

He would fill empty milk bottles with the oil and then stack them in neat rows on the shelves in the huge walk-in pantry. Soon the shelves were filled with over fifty quarts of Papa's precious olive oil.

One late afternoon, Jean Louis, who was now ten months old, was crawling around the apartment looking for some mischief to get into. He found it. Someone left the pantry door open. Naturally, Jean-Louis crawled in and closed the door behind him.

The bottles of oil immediately caught his eye. He was particularly fascinated with the Gluk! Gluk! sound the bottles made when he emptied them.

Gluk! Gluk! Gluk! He emptied one bottle after another. Soon the floor was flooded with two inches of oil. The oil found its way under the pantry door and formed an oil slick in the hallway.

Fifteen minutes went by, before Mom and Ginette noticed that Jean-Louis was missing.

"Ginette, pou einai o Jean Louis?"

"Je ne sais pas, Mama."

"Jean-Louis! Jean-Louis!" they called out.

They spotted the oil slick and when they opened the pantry door, they discovered the disaster. Jean-Louis was covered with oil. Twenty empty quart bottles were scattered on the floor.

Mom and Ginette quickly scooped up Jean-Louis, dumped him into the bathtub, turned on the water and rushed back to clean up the mess in the pantry.

At that precise moment, Papa came home. When he saw the empty bottles and the two inches of oil on the pantry floor, he cried out, "Who spilled my oil?"

The whole house shook. Avon Avenue shook. All of Newark, New Jersey trembled. The seismograph at Fordham University registered 8.5 on the Richter Scale. The following report went out on the wires: **MAJOR EARTHQUAKE HITS NEWARK, N.J.!!**

Mom and Ginette pleaded with Papa as he slid toward the bathroom.

"Don't hurt him! He's only a baby!"

"Oui!"

"He didn't know what he was doing!"

"Oui, oui!"

When Papa reached the bathroom, he saw Jean-Louis sitting in the bath tub happily splashing the water. His little fat body glistened with oil. When he saw Papa, he laughed and stretched out his oily arms to be picked up. Papa picked up Jean-Louis, hugged him, and smothered him with kisses.

"You are truly a Greek!" he said to Jean-Louis. "Your father didn't have sense enough to have you oiled! So, you went and did it yourself!"

After that, Papa never dropped Jean-Louis again.

Mama and My Guns

In the last weeks of World War II, the German army was rapidly retreating from the Russians. They knew the war was practically over and were quite anxious to be taken prisoner by the Americans rather than the Russians.

During this time I was in Company A, 54th Signal Airborne Battalion attached to the First Allied Airborne Army. We had jumped across the Rhine River and were heading northwest to hook up with the Russian Army. That's when my company of 200 men ran into two German infantry divisions of 20,000 men begging us to take them prisoner. Naturally, we obliged.

The captain gave me the job of disarming all of the German officers. They would politely ask me where to put their weapons and I would tell them to toss them in a pile I had started.

In a few hours, over a thousand Lugers, P38s, Italian Barettas, and other beautifully crafted pistols were piled twenty feet high. I didn't waste any time emptying my beat-up duffel bag and filling it with 125 priceless pistols.

The duffel bag weighed over 150 pounds and I had no idea how I was going to get it from Germany to Newark, New Jersey.

It was six months before I was discharged. Six months of delicate negotiations and sheer brute force. A shakedown inspection marked each step of the way.

The first inspection was pulled when we returned to our base in France, the next one at Camp Lucky Strike, where we waited to board a troop ship. We had countless other inspections while crossing the Atlantic and at Fort Devens, Massachusetts, where we were debriefed and finally discharged.

All in all, it cost me 15 guns, $2000 in cash, and a brand new pair of jump boots to get that duffel bag past all those inspections.

Free at last, I dragged my duffel bag onto a bus to Boston, then onto a train to Newark, and finally into a taxi. When I arrived at 245 Avon Avenue where my mother and father lived, I knew the trip was over.

My mother had gone shopping, so Mr. Fader, the landlord, let me in. We never met, but he knew who I was. (We lived on Plane Street when I left for the Army four years before.)

I checked out the apartment and soon discovered a huge walk-in pantry with a high ceiling. A perfect place to display my 110 priceless hand guns.

I didn't waste any time finding a hammer and some nails. By the time my mother came home, I had all my guns hanging in nice neat rows on the walls of her pantry.

Six months later, Ginette, my French war bride, arrived in the states with my son, Jean-Louis.

There was no room to store my guns in our new apartment, so I left them hanging on the walls in Mama's pantry. I wasn't a bit worried. I knew they would be perfectly safe there.

One day, I dropped by Mother's to oil my guns. (I didn't want them to get rusty.) When I opened the pantry door, all I saw were 110 empty nails on the walls and no guns!

"Mama!" I shouted, "What happened to my guns?"

"Guns?" she asks. "Ah yes... The guns! I meant to tell you, but I forgot."

"Tell me what, Mama?" I was crying.

"You know Mr. Fader, the landlord?"

"Yeah?"

"You know, he and his wife are Jewish."

"So?"

"Well, two weeks ago he came up and asked if we had any guns we could donate to Israel."

"Israel?"

"He told me how they needed guns to fight for their independence. You know, the way we Greeks fought the Turks for our independence."

"It's not the same, Mama."

"Anyway, he couldn't believe his eyes when I showed him your guns."

"Oh, no."

"He asked if he could take one. I told him he could take them all."

"No, no..."

"I never saw Mr. Fader so excited. He needed something to put the guns in, so I gave him that dirty old green bag you brought home from the Army."

"Mama! How could you do this to me?"

"Listen," she says, "those people need those guns a lot more than you do."

I learned a long time ago, never to argue with Mama. Especially, when it's a done deal.

The Apollo

My father's life-long dream was to own the biggest and best restaurant in downtown Newark. "We will call it the Apollo," he would say, and it will be opened 24 hour a day.

He had it all figured out. If we could raise five hundred dollars, the restaurant and food vendors promised to kick in the rest to help get him started. These arrangements were common during the Depression. Each week, we would gather around Papa at the kitchen table as he emptied the coffee can and counted the money we had saved thus far.

All through the Depression we struggled to raise that 500 dollars. Ever since I was eight years old I worked. I shined shoes, sold newspapers, set up pins in bowling alleys, delivered groceries, worked as a movie usher, and every penny I made, I gave to Papa to put into that coffee can.

Each year we would get closer and closer to our goal, then some catastrophe would wipe out all our savings and we would start from scratch again.

When I graduated from high school in Jun,e 1941, I immediately got a fulltime job at Western Electric. On payday, I proudly turned over my first week's salary to Papa. The family gathered around the kitchen table as he slowly counted the money I had given him. When he announced the total amount, seventeen dollars and fifty cents, the family cheered.

He gave me fifty cents to keep and put the rest into the old coffee can.

"*Bravo, Yiannaki.* " he said proudly. "Can you get your sister a job there?"

"Yeah, they're hiring coil winders on the ninth floor."

"Good." Papa then turned to my sister, "*Eleni,* no more school. Tomorrow morning you will go with your brother and get a job."

The following week, Papa counted two salaries and within a few months the coffee can was filled to the top. We had finally raised the five hundred dollars.

At the time, we lived on Plane Street in Newark, which was near downtown. Papa used the five hundred dollars to convert a small empty store downstairs into Louie's Luncheonette. He managed to squeeze in a counter with eight stools, and six tables and chairs for four.

Papa did the cooking, my brothers, Constantine and Babe worked behind the counter and waited on the tables, and Mom took cash. They all worked without pay, thus keeping the overhead to a minimum. Helen and I continued to work at Western Electric to support the family.

Every penny Papa made from Louie's Luncheonette went into the bank. He was determined to save enough money to make his lifelong dream of opening the Apollo come true.

Historical events soon made this possible. Japan bombed Pearl Harbor and the United States entered the war. The War Department took over the Prudential Building, which was a block away from Papa's luncheonette and installed it's ODB (Office of Dependents Benefits) operation there. Thousands of office workers worked there around the clock making benefit payments to the dependents of service men and women.

Many of these workers were black and ate in Louie's Luncheonette because the food was hot, tasty, and plentiful. Papa installed a juke box and filled it with Dinah Washington and Billy Ekstine records. The place soon had the reputation of catering to blacks. The whites stayed away, but that didn't bother Papa a bit. The blacks were good customers and they ate and tipped well.

Meanwhile, I had joined the Army and was overseas when Papa made his big move. Louie's Luncheonette made him a lot of money. He sold it and opened the Apollo on Washington and Academy Streets in the heart of downtown Newark. It was exactly the way Papa had described it to us so many times.

It was a huge, modern restaurant occupying almost an entire block. It was open 24 hours a day and required three shifts of waitresses, bus boys, countermen, cooks, and kitchen help.

Soon after Papa opened the Apollo, my brother, Constantine was drafted. Papa was left Mama, my sister, and Babe, who was still in school, to run the place.

It was hard to find good help in those days. People made a lot more money working in the shipyards than working in a restaurant. Papa was forced to work two and many times, three shifts in the kitchen without rest.

The news from overseas had a devastating effect on his health. On Christmas Day in 1944, he received a telegram from the Defense Department that reported me missing in action during the Battle of the Bulge.

After that, he received another telegram that Constantine was seriously wounded on his first day in combat crossing the Metz River in Germany and was recovering in a hospital somewhere in England.

Other Greek families in Newark were receiving similar telegrams about their sons. Peter Boucouvalas was critically wounded on D Day in Normandy.

Johnny Johnson's father had a fatal heart attack when he received a telegram, which he never opened, congratulating him because his son had won the Flying Cross medal for heroism.

Our fathers, who fought alongside their fathers in the wars against the Turks and Bulgars, were turned away by the American recruiters when they volunteered to fight alongside their sons.

Our parents suffered additional grief when they were cut off from their beloved families in Greece. For years, they didn't know if their mothers and fathers were dead or alive.

After the war, letters from the villages trickled back to us describing the holocaust the Greeks had suffered during the war. Both Mama and Papa received letters from their villages explaining how their parents perished during the war.

When Constantine and I finally came home, we were stunned to see how much Papa had aged and how seriously ill he was. At forty-five, he was an old man.

We immediately sold the Apollo and brought him to Maine where he regained his health and spent most of his time doing what he loved best: fishing. He died five years later.

The struggle to achieve a lifelong dream and then to have that dream destroy you is a classic Greek tragedy that has been repeated many times in the Greek diaspora.

Chapter Eight

Return to Greece

Who Am I?

When I worked at Bell Telephone Laboratories, I was a 100 percent, certified, class A workaholic. My job consumed me 24 hours a day, and I had no time to think of anything else. I brought home work to do every night and on weekends. At the end of each year, I would lose the vacation days I had coming to me because I couldn't find the time during the year to take off for a vacation.

I even looked like a workaholic. My curly hair was always cropped short, and I wore horn-rimmed bifocals. My God, I looked like Henry Kissinger!

Then, it happened. A management consultant firm had convinced our top management that the company's executives would become better managers if they got in touch with themselves. Well, I was chosen as one of the fifteen executives who were to participate in the first two-week seminar in Ocean City, New Jersey.

They told us that the best way to get in touch with ourselves was to keep asking ourselves "Who am I?" The seminar was very successful. Most of us got in touch with ourselves. Five executives quit their jobs outright, four divorced their wives, and another decided to take a sabbatical to sail around the world in a 35-foot sailboat.

Me? I still wasn't sure who I was. So, I decided to go to Greece for six weeks and find out. As soon as I got home from the seminar, I called my mother.

"Hello, Ma. *Ego ime, o Yiannis.* (It's me, Johnnie.) Give me Uncle Thoma's address. Friday, I'm going to Greece."

This came out of the blue, like a bolt of lightning since I had never shown any interest in visiting Greece before.

She was crying. This would be the first time that someone from our family was returning to Greece after fifty years.

And that is how in 1967, I decided to visit Greece. Mama had not seen her older brother, Thoma, since she left Greece as a young girl. And Papa always dreamed of going back to see his mother and father, but sadly, that dream vanished when they perished during the war. Papa died without ever returning to his beloved village. I somehow felt that I was now going in his place.

The flight to Athens took 10 hours, which gave me plenty of time to think about the relatives I was about to visit. Uncle Thoma, a dentist who lived in Piraeus, was the first one on my list.

I had once asked Aunt Mary why Uncle Thoma was left behind when our family came to America. Besides being thorough, Aunt Mary liked to start all her stories from the very beginning. So, she started by telling me about the incident that led to her mother and father's (our grandparents') marriage.

In 1875, Stavros Kyriakakos (our great-grandfather) married Politime and lived in the small mountain village of *Lukadeka* in the *Mani*. They had three children, Alkiviades (our grandfather), Essasios, and Evangelia.

When the children were small their mother died, and their father, Stavros, remarried. His second wife gave birth to another child. (This is when Aunt Mary finally got to the incident in her story.)

Late one summer afternoon while a violent thunderstorm was brewing, Stavros climbed to the roof of his tower-like stone house to look for the children who were out herding their flock of goats. His young wife was sitting in the doorway feeding the baby while talking to a neighbor. A bolt of lightning suddenly ripped out of the black sky and struck Stavros and then streaked down the side of the tower and into the doorway, killing the baby and severely burning the young mother.

Her family immediately slaughtered a cow, skinned it, and covered her body with its wet skin. They then took her back to their home where she recovered. (Aunt Mary's stories were always filled with details.)

Mortally injured, Stavros lived long enough to make his brother Nichola promise to care for his three orphaned children. Since Nichola had a large family of his own to care for, caring for another three children presented him with additional problems.

So when Alkiviades approached his 16th birthday, Uncle Nichola decided it was time to marry him off to some woman who would take care of him as well as his smaller brother and sister. He searched high and low for just the right woman. He finally found her in a nearby village, *Chimara*.

Her name was Eleni Thomakos who had a reputation for being so tough that no one would marry her regardless of how big the *prika* (dowry) was. Eleni was twenty-three and was classified as a hopeless spinster. A perfect match for our hapless 16-year-old grandfather.

Uncle Nichola wasted no time in paying a social call on Eleni's father, Papa Thomakos, the village priest with a large family which included five daughters. After a few glasses of wine, Nichola made a proposition that Papa Thomakos could not refuse. And that's how our grandparents were married.

Alkiviades and Eleni settled in a small, single-room, stone house in *Lukadeka*, and in time, they managed to have four children, Leonidas, Mary, Thoma, and Ahlayia (our mother).

In 1907, Alkiviades came to Lowell, Massachusetts to work in the mills. A year later he went to work in the Buck Mills in Lewiston, Maine. Alkiviades regularly sent a large portion of his pay back home to help support his family.

In 1911, the money suddenly stopped coming, as did Alkiviades' letters. Worried that he had taken up with a younger woman, Eleni left her two youngest children, Ahlayia and Thoma, in the care of Uncle Nichola and took Leonidas and Mary with her to the United States to find their father. When she arrived on Ellis Island, the immigration official would not let Eleni and her children get off the ship because she didn't have the proper papers.

Through an interpreter she gave the official her word, that if he didn't let her off the boat to find her husband, she would jump into the water and drown herself, thus leaving behind two orphans to be cared for.

"She can't do that!" the official protested.

"Ah, but she will," replied the interpreter. "If she gives her word to do something, she will do it. She's a *Maniatisa!*"

"She's crazy!"

"Same thing, sir."

A cousin, Michael Kyriakakos, came to her rescue, and the immigration officials allowed Eleni to disembark.

When Eleni arrived in Lewiston, Maine, she found her husband serving time in jail. It seems that some Albanian made the mistake of calling Alkiviades a liar. My grandfather pulled out his penknife and a fight ensued. Alkiviades was arrested and charged with aggravated assault and battery.

In court, he argued, "Nobody calls a *Maniati* a liar and gets away with it. It was a matter of honor."

The judge didn't buy it and sentenced him to six months in jail.

Eleni Kyriakakos applied the same diplomatic reasoning with the Lewiston judge as she did with the immigration official and had her husband released in her cognizance. As soon as Alkiviades was released from jail, he went back to work and raised enough money to send for Ahlayia, and Thoma.

However, according to Aunt Mary, Uncle Nichola was reluctant to send both children to the United States because Alkiviades and his family would probably never come back to Greece. So, he sent Ahlayia and held on to Thoma as an inducement for their return.

Three years later, Alkiviades moved his family from Lewiston to Saco, Maine where years later, my mother and father were married and I was born.

"Please fasten your seat belts," the stewardess's voice gently awakened me. "We're about to land."

I fastened my seat belt and looked out the small window to see for the first time the beautiful Acropolis in the distance.

Since no one knew I was coming, there was no one to greet me when my plane landed in Athens. So, I hailed a taxi and gave the driver my uncle's address in Piraeus. In less than twenty minutes, I was ringing my Uncle Thoma's doorbell. When the buzzer sounded, I pushed in the door and entered the hallway. Uncle Thoma appeared on the second floor landing in his white coat holding a pair of dental pliers.

I recognized him right away from the pictures we had of him, but he had no idea who the man was standing in the hallway with two suitcases.

"Who are you?" he asked.

"Yianni Kaloyerinis," I said in Greek.

Being that it's a Greek custom to name the firstborn son after the paternal grandfather, I have three first cousins named *Yianni Kaloyerinis* and Uncle Thoma knew them all.

"I know all the *Yianni Kaloyerinithes.* I've worked on their teeth," he said, "but I don't know you."

I laughed and told him, "I'm your sister Ahlayia's son, *Yianni.*"

When he heard that he tossed his dental pliers into the air and ran down the stairs to greet me. Tears were in his eyes as he brought me upstairs. He immediately dismissed the woman patient who was sitting in the dental chair waiting to have her tooth extracted and brought me into his apartment to greet Aunt Mimi.

Soon my cousins, Alkiviades and Lela, arrived, and all the neighbors gathered to greet me. Greeks are such a warm, friendly, and curious people, just the way the Greeks are in America.

"What kind of job do you have?"

"Does it pay well?"

"Why didn't you bring your wife?"

After the neighbors left, we settled down to tell family stories. Uncle Thoma was a great story teller, and I especially enjoyed listening to stories about Mama and Aunt Mary when they were little girls growing up in Greece.

My cousins laughed at the way I told my stories in Greek, especially when I used Greek words that didn't exist in Greece. These were American words that were twisted by our parents to make them sound Greek. They used *"roofie"* for "roof" and *"busie"* for "bus" and *"spitalia"* for "hospital", etc.

It took very little time for Uncle Thoma and I to become close friends. I felt as though I had known him all my life because Mama and Aunt Mary talked about him all the time.

They were proud of the way Thoma, who grew up in a small mountain village in the *Mani,* became a lawyer and a dentist. The man was not only highly educated in both professions, he was also an expert in Greek history, philosophy, and culture.

"Your Uncle Thoma is a true *Maniati!*" Aunt Mary would say before telling us the story about how he earned his law degree and passed the Greek bar exam, and how he hung out his shingle and greeted his first client. When Thoma learned that he was obligated to defend a client who might be guilty, he gave up the practice of law and went back to the university and became a dentist.

It was getting late, so we made plans for the next day. Uncle Thoma and Aunt Mimi would accompany me to the *Mani* and we would leave early tomorrow morning.

When I went to bed that night, I fell asleep for the first time in Greece feeling good about myself and who I was. A Greek-American with a proud heritage rooted in Greece.

The next morning Uncle Thoma and Aunt Mimi were packed and ready to go. I told Uncle Thoma that I was going to Athens to rent a car from Hertz.

"What kind of car?" he asked.

"I don't know. Whatever they give me, I guess."

"How much is it going to cost?"

"The travel agent said that I could probably get a brand-new car for about thirty-five dollars a day, plus a little extra per mile and for insurance. The whole thing shouldn't cost more than $350 to $400 a week."

"What?" My uncle almost had a heart attack. "Are you crazy?"

"Why, what's wrong?" I asked.

"Too much!" responded my uncle.

(Oh. Oh. I thought that sure sounds a lot like my mother when I was a little boy and she used to take me shopping with her!)

"I know a man who owns two cars that he rents out. He does his business in the *kafeneo* (coffee house)."

"Good!" I said. "Can we see him now?"

"No!" Uncle Thoma said with undue caution, "It's much better I see him alone."

"Oh, Okay! When will you see him?"

"I will see him this morning and I will negotiate a much better deal for you."

"Negotiate? How long will that take?"

93

Uncle Thoma held up two fingers and said, "One or maybe two days."

"That long?" I said with a certain disappointment.

"We must not let him think that we are in a hurry."

The negotiations lasted four full days. Uncle Thoma was extremely proud of the deal he made and the amount of money he saved me.

"We got the better car for only five dollars a day with no extra charges."

"Wow!" I said, "that's some deal. But what about the insurance?"

"We don't need any."

"Why not?"

"We pay for any damages that we cause and he pays for anything that goes wrong with the car that's not our fault."

"Sounds reasonable to me. Did you and he sign a paper agreeing to that?"

"Didn't have to. He gave me his word and I gave him mine."

I couldn't believe my eyes when I went to pick up the car. It was a tiny, old, beat-up two-door Fiat sport coupe. If this was the better car of the two, I would hate to see the condition of the other car.

I squeezed into the front seat and checked out the dashboard. Uncle Thoma kicked the tires to make sure they had plenty of air in them.

"Uncle Thoma, did you know that this car does not have any air conditioning?"

"That's alright! We will keep the windows open."

"And the windshield wipers don't work!"

"We won't need them! It never rains in the *Mani* in July and August."

"The floorboard has a big hole in it. I can see the ground!"

"So, We'll cover it with newspapers."

"Uncle Thoma, the hand brake is missing!"

"Yes, and I already told him about it. So, we won't get blamed for losing it when we bring the car back."

Being that I was the only one who could drive, I sat in the driver's seat. Aunt Mimi was squashed into the backseat and Uncle Thoma sat up front with me. I almost broke the handle rolling down the window to be ready with my hand signal when I pulled out. Uncle Thoma was filled with excitement and anticipation.

"Well, how do you like the car?" he asked.

"It's beautiful, Uncle Thoma. Beautiful!" I said, amazed at the amount of black smoke that was pouring out of the tailpipe.

I noticed Aunt Mimi crossing herself over and over again while whispering a prayer. As we pulled out, I also crossed myself. I figured we were going to need all the help we could get on this trip.

The MANI

Disaster on a Mountain Top

We left Piraeus and headed south towards the *Mani* which is a mountainous area located on the southern tip of the Peloponnesian Peninsula.

We stopped for our first break when we crossed the Corinth Canal. When we were ready to move on I suggested that Aunt Mimi change seats with Uncle Thoma for awhile. They both rejected my suggestion, so we continued our trip as before. (I later learned that the Greek custom was that men sit in the front and women in the back.)

The closer we got to the *Mani,* the worst the roads became. All the roads below Sparta were unpaved with most of the dirt and gravel washed away during the winter rains. The roads were filled with outcroppings of rocks that jutted six inches or more above the ground.

The Fiat had no back springs, and with Aunt Mimi sitting in the backseat, the bottom of the car barely cleared the road by two inches. This meant that if we could not skirt around these outcroppings, we would have to stop the car and pull Aunt Mimi out of the backseat. I would then slowly drive over the rocks.

We had to help Aunt Mimi struggle to get in and out of the car because the frontseat was jammed and wouldn't move or bend forward. Aunt Mimi was a real trooper and never complained when we pulled her out or pushed her into the car.

After doing this a dozen times, we came upon another outcropping of rocks.

"Aren't you going to stop?" Uncle Thoma asked.

I didn't have the heart to pull Aunt Mimi out of that backseat again. She was exhausted and covered with dust that was coming up through the broken floorboard.

"I think we can make it if we drive over it very slow" I said.

Everyone held their breath as I did just that.

We were almost across when I said, "It's going to be close, but I think we're going to make it!"

CREWUNCHH!

We all closed our eyes when we heard the sickening sound of a steel gas tank being ripped apart.

When I looked under the car, I saw gasoline dripping out of a small opening in the seam of the gas tank.

I looked around us and I saw that we were totally isolated on top of a mountain. There was nothing but mountains and miles of rocks and boulders surrounding us. The only sound that could be heard was the hot wind and some crow laughing at our predicament.

I looked down and saw a puddle of gasoline forming under the car.

"Is it bad?" Uncle Thoma asked.

"It's a disaster" I said in English because I couldn't find the right Greek word to express my feeling at that moment.

"*Yianni*, should I get out of the car?" Aunt Mimi called out from the backseat of the car.

"It's okay, Aunt Mimi. Stay there."

I took the gum I was chewing and covered the small opening with it. It seemed to work, so we took off as quickly as possible, hoping to find a garage in the next village.

We coasted three miles down the mountainside and entered a small village. I stopped and checked the gas tank and discovered that the gum had fallen off, and the gasoline was leaking again.

I frantically asked an old woman if there was a garage closeby. "*Ohi!* (no!)" she said and pointed to a small bicycle shop.

At the shop, we were greeted by the owner who was a young man in his early twenties.

He smiled and asked us, "What's the problem?"

I told him what had happened and that he had to remove the tank, empty the gasoline, and weld the crack in the seam without blowing us up.

He looked under the car and examined the leaking gas tank. He stood up, smiled, and told us not to worry.

"Taki!" he called out.

A small boy appeared out of nowhere. The young man gave him a drachma coin and told him to buy a *loukoumi* at the village store.

A *loukoumi* is a Turkish candy made out of pure sugar (much like our gum drops). It is about two square inches in size, extremely sticky and covered with confectionery sugar. It will not melt in your mouth, and it is virtually impossible to chew on a *loukoumi* without getting most of it stuck between your teeth.

In a few seconds, Taki was back and gave the young man the *loukoumi* he bought. The young man softened the *loukoumi* with his two hands (the way a pitcher uses both hands to rub a new baseball).

He then crawled under the car and covered the cracked seam of the gas tank with the *loukoumi*.

I asked him, "Are you sure the *loukoumi* will hold up?"

He laughed and said, "The entire car will fall apart before that *loukoumi* falls off."

He refused to accept any money for such a simple job. We shook hands and left the village.

Every time we stopped after that, I would check to see if the gas tank was leaking. The *loukoumi* was still there, sealing the open seam, just the way he said it would. In time, the *loukoumi* was covered with so much dirt and dust that it became part of the car.

To this day, every time I am in a Greek home and I am served a *loukoumi*, I think about the *loukoumi* that saved us after the disaster we had on that mountaintop.

Mama's Village: Lukadeka

We were only a few kilometers from Mama's village, *Lukadeka*. Each time we drove through or passed a tiny mountain village, Uncle Thoma would tell me the name of the village and the family or families that came from there.

He would point to a village nestled in a mountain valley and say, "That's *Kavalli*. The *Boucouvallis* family comes from there."

It was amazing, practically every Greek family I knew came from the *Mani*.

A few minutes later, we were driving through a village, and he would point to a tower-like house and say, "This is *Chimara* and that's the house your grandmother was born in."

Aunt Mimi, sitting quietly in the backseat, suddenly announced, "And this is *Lukadeka*, your mother's village."

"Stop the car," Uncle Thoma announced. "We are here!"

"And that is the house your mother, Uncle Thoma, Aunt Mary, and Uncle Leonides were born in" Aunt Mimi said pointing to a small, single-room stone house perched on the side of a hill.

It was in good condition because Uncle Thoma maintained it as a summer home. The house, like all the others in the village, was built out of harsh, jagged gray rocks and boulders that dominated everything. The harshness was punctuated by a constant wind that whistled relentlessly.

"Come, I will show you where your *Papoo* and *Yiayia* (grandparents) are buried." Uncle Thoma signaled me to follow him.

I had a difficult time keeping up with him as I stumbled up the crooked rock-strewn pathway leading to the top of the hill. The wind began to howl as I approached the top. The other side of the hill was covered with a blanket of a million sweet-smelling lavender flowers.

"There!" Uncle Thoma pointed to two, small, white marble crosses gently glistening in the sunlight halfway down the lavender hillside.

I knelt next to their graves and crossed myself. I remembered when they came to Newark to visit us for a week before returning to Greece to live with Uncle Thoma and Aunt Mimi.

And here they are now, I thought, laying side by side in a beautiful bed of sweet smelling lavender flowers. I could still hear them telling us stories that made us all laugh so much.

"I love you, *Yiayia*. I love you, *Papoo*" I whispered. I wiped away my tears and crossed myself.

When we returned to the house, we were warmly greeted by the villagers and the village priest.

"Who is the stranger?" an old woman whispered.

"It's Ahlayia's son from America."

The old woman's eyes filled with tears as she crossed herself. "Our beautiful little *Ahlathie* (pear) was a child when she left us and now her son, a *palekarie* (handsome young man), has returned. Praise the Lord!"

"It is a miracle."

The young priest firmly shook my hand. His grip was strong and the face behind his heavy black beard was as rugged as the rock strewn terrain.

"It is truly a miracle," he said as he smiled, "you have arrived on the same day that the bishop is coming to our village."

The priest then thanked me for the bronze chalice and vestments that our family had donated to the village church after Mama's brother, Papa Leonides (the priest), had passed away. At that precise moment the church bell started to clang. Clang ! Clang!

"The bishop has arrived!" everyone shouted.

The villagers rushed towards the church.

"The bishop has arrived!"

I immediately started unloading the car.

Uncle Thoma grabbed me by the arm "Come on, let's go. The bishop has arrived!"

"I know, I know, but I have to unload the car first."

"Why?"

"The car doors don't lock and these cameras are very expensive. Someone might steal them," I explained.

He laughed and said, "*Vrai,* if you stuck thousand-drachma bills under the windshield wipers, no one would touch them! You are in *Mani!*"

"Oh," I said. "Okay. Let's go!"

When I entered the small church, it was like I was stepping back five hundred years in time. I had never been in a church like this before. The women and children sat on the clay floor in the front of the altar. The men sat in high chairs placed along the back wall and two sides of the church. I was given the honor of sitting in the chair in the back of the room facing the altar.

After the bishop completed mass, he delivered his sermon to the villagers in simple Greek. Even I understood every word he said.

"God is everywhere
  He is in the water you drink,
  the air you breathe
  and in the food you eat.
  He is with you when you tend
  to your goats,
  and pick your olives.
  You are never alone.
  God is with you always."

There was something poetic and hypnotic about the way he spoke.

Outside, the sun went down and darkness set in. Soon the inside of the church became dark. The only light came from the candles stuck in the sand-filled container next to the icon of *Panayia* (Mother Mary).

I kept wondering why someone didn't turned on the lights. It suddenly occurred to me that they didn't have electricity. Everything was just as it had been for hundreds of years .

When the service ended, we returned to Uncle Thoma's house where the neighbors brought us delicious food to eat and wine to drink. We spent half the night telling stories.

102

I heard five different versions of how Mama fell into an abandoned well and how she took off without telling anyone that the man who climbed down to rescue her was stuck and couldn't get out.

After they left, I laid down on a straw matress and listened to the wind whistling outside. I fell asleep thinking that this was the same wind Mama listened to when she slept here as a little girl.

Baptism in *Mani*

After my visit to my mother's village, we moved on to Kotrona, a small village closeby. Uncle Thoma and Aunt Mimi had planned to visit Niko, a cousin who lived there.

As we approached the village, Uncle Thoma told me what to expect. He explained that many years ago, Niko had been arrested for a crime he did not commit. Niko spent ten years in jail and was released when new evidence was uncovered that proved him innocent. But alas, despite this turn of events, no Greek family would consider Niko suitable to marry their daughter. Finally, a family from a distant village agreed to let Niko marry their young daughter who everyone believed was slightly retarded.

"So, what happened?" I asked.

"Since then, they had a son who is perfectly normal."

"*Thoxas o Theo!* (Thank God!)," Aunt Mimi cried out from the backseat as she crossed herself.

"And now, they have an infant daughter."

"She's the one I'm going to baptize as soon as we get there!" Aunt Mimi said proudly, showing me the two white candles that she bought in Piraeus.

"Ah! Here we are!" Uncle Thoma announced.

Niko and his young son welcomed us as we entered their home. Uncle Thoma introduced me to the villagers that had gathered there.

"This is my nephew, my sister Ahlayia's son, and he's from America."

Everyone was quite impressed.

Aunt Mimi picked up a beautiful infant from a homemade crib.

"And this is Maria." she said. "The little girl we are going to soon baptize."

"What a beautiful child!" I said. "I am looking forward to going to church and seeing her baptized."

Suddenly, everyone became strangely quiet. The silence was broken by Uncle Thoma.

"No. No. You really don't want to go."

"Why not?" I asked.

"Uncle Thoma looked at his feet and said, "Here in *Mani*, only women go to a girl's baptism."

"What if it were a boy?"

"Oh, that's different."

"Everyone would go to church."

"The Godfather would give a feast for the entire village with food, music, and everything!"

"Well," I smiled defiantly and said, "I am going to go to see Maria baptized."

A young woman took Maria from Aunt Mimi and quietly approached me. This must be the baby's mother, I thought.

"Excuse me, kind and gentle stranger," she said, "please put both your hands on my daughter, so she can be blessed forever."

Morning Ritual

After spending a week in the harsh rock-strewn *Mani*, Uncle Thoma, Aunt Mimi and I headed for the *Vatica*, the eastern prong of the Peloponessian Peninsular. Our plan was to visit Uncle Steve, Papa's only surviving brother, who lived in *Neapolis*.

Neapolis is a fishing village with a ferry that takes people, farm animals, cars, trucks, and anything else, regularly to and from the ancient island of Kithera (the birthplace of Aphrodite).

This is where Uncle Steve chose to build his villa when he retired to Greece. It combined the features of a suburban split-level ranch house in New Jersey with those of a mountain village farm house in the *Vatica*.

Although their dreams came true when they returned to their beloved Greece after working in a foreign country most of their lives, they were not the same Greeks they were when they left.

The first thing Uncle Steve did each morning was proudly hang a large Greek flag from a flagpole permanently mounted on one side of his second floor balcony. And then, with equal pride, he would hang an equally large American flag from a flagpole mounted on the other side of his balcony.

These two flags represented the affection he had for both Greece, his birthplace, and America where he worked for over fifty years in his shoe-shine and hat-cleaning establishment in Newark's Penn Station.

After hanging out his flags, Uncle Steve would slowly dress, wearing a white shirt, a thin black tie, a light vest and sparkling shiny black shoes. He would finally put on his Panama straw hat, check himself in the mirror, take his cane and slowly walk towards the *Plaka* (town square).

As Uncle Steve approached the *Plaka*, George, another older Greek, was approaching the *Plaka* from the other end of town. George had worked as a cook for over fifty years in Chicago. He and Uncle Steve were childhood friends, now retired and living in *Neapolis*. Every day they would meet in the *Plaka* and greet each other in English.

"Good Morning, George."

"Good Morning, Steve."

"How are you this morning?"

"Fine and you?"

They would then sit at a table and continue their conversation in English. From time to time they would have to search for the correct word.

They did this every morning because they did not want to forget the language they struggled so hard to learn while living and working in America for fifty years.

Papa's Village: *Misohori*

If you look up at the mountain that is behind the town of *Neapolis*, you will see my father's village, *Misohori*. As a small boy, Papa used to walk down that mountainside to *Neapolis* where he worked on the fishing boats or fished with his father and brothers. They would stay out at sea for weeks at a time. Papa had never forgotten how to knit the kind of fishing nets they used on those trips.

Although Uncle Steve told me there was nothing to see in *Misohori* and that only a few people still lived there, I insisted on going there.

The village was only a mile up the mountain (as the crow flies); however, the winding road that would take us there was eight miles long. So, we all piled into the Fiat and headed for *Misohori*. Uncle Steve insisted on sitting in the front with me and Uncle Thoma.

The extra weight, crowded conditions, sharp turns, and knowing that I had no hand brake made the driving somewhat difficult. The Fiat huffed and puffed, leaving a trail of black smoke as it climbed up the eight miles of winding dirt road.

I almost went off the road when we passed a huge castle perched on a castro about one hundred yards to the side of us.

"Look!" I cried out, "A castle!"

"Keep your eye on the road, Yianni!"

I remembered Papa telling us stories about that castle. It belonged to the Venetians who were there for over four hundred years. When we asked him why the Greeks allowed them to stay there so long, he would tell us that the Venetians kept the Turks away. When the Turks were no longer a problem, the Greeks got rid of the Venetians by cutting off their water supply.

When we reached the village, we were warmly greeted by the few villagers that still lived there. The older people remembered Papa as a young boy who loved to sing. One old lady referred to him as *O micros o nafties!* (the little sailor).

They too were all great storytellers. They enjoyed telling stories about my grandfather, *Yianni Kaloyerinis*. He was tall and handsome with a fine head of hair. He had the reputation of being the best hunter and fisherman in the area. The villagers claimed that the King Constantine of Greece would come to the Vatica specifically to go hunting with my grandfather.

At the time, this story sounded a bit far-fetched. Today, I see it in a different light since then Vice-President Bush invited my sister's son, Louis, to go fishing with him off the coast of Maine.

Bush's invitation had nothing to do with Louis's ability to fish. Louis just happened to be the executive editor of Maine's leading newspapers.

I learned a lot about my father from the villagers. He was born in in *Misohori* in 1897 and was 17 years old when he joined the Greek navy in 1914. Of course, they told me many of the same stories I had heard from Papa.

While I was visiting *Misohori*, I saw a tall cyprus tree hanging over a 1000-foot cliff at the edge of the village.

Papa once told me a story of how angry his mother became when she saw him climbing up a tall cyprus tree that hung over a 1000-foot cliff at the edge of his village. He was eight years old at the time and wanted to see if a nest located at the top of the tree contained any eggs.

Papa laughed, "I finally reached the nest and there were no eggs in it! Ach! When I came down from the tree, my mother gave me a spanking that I have not forgotten to this day."

Could this be the tree that Papa climbed I wondered?

The top of the tree swayed back and forth in the breeze as if it were trying to tell me something.

I looked up and there it was! There I saw the nest, exactly the way Papa described it to me when I was eight years old!

As I walked around the village, I had this strange feeling that I had been there before.

I thought about the way Papa dreamed of coming back to his beloved village some day. He never did. And now I was there in his place.

Are You Crazy?
The Turks Will Kill You!

When we returned to Piraeus, I told Uncle Thoma, that I was going to Turkey for a few days to visit a friend.

"Are you crazy? " he cried out in shock. "The Turks will kill you!"

"Why would they want to do that?" I asked.

"When they find out you are Greek, they will cut your throat, and dump your body into the Bosphorus."

"My friend will not let anything like that happen."

"You can never trust a Turk! Never!"

"I trust my friend."

Uncle Thoma crossed himself. "*Panayia mou!* My nephew has completely lost his mind."

We argued like this for over an hour before Uncle Thoma finally gave up when he realized that, regardless of what he said, I would not change my mind.

"When are you leaving?" he asked quietly.

"I'm flying out of Athens tomorrow."

"That's not possible! No Greek airplane would ever fly to Turkey. Not after what they did to us in Cyprus."

"I'm flying Air France."

"Where will you stay?"

"In the finest hotel in Turkey with a beautiful view of the Bosphorus."

"Beautiful, my foot! It is most likely overridden with rats, lice, and roaches."

Early the next morning, my plane landed in Turkey without incident.

Once I got past customs, I boarded the hotel bus that was waiting for me. An hour after I left Greece, I was unpacking my bag in the heart of Turkey.

Early that afternoon, I went to visit my friend, Tosun Barak, who lived on the other side of the Bosphorus. In order to get to his home, I had to go eight miles south, cross the only bridge that spanned the Bosphorus, and then travel eight miles north.

To do this, I took a *Dolmush*, which is a Turkish cross between a mini-bus and a taxi. Actually, they are large ambulances with several rows of seats added in the back. They have no identification lights or signs. However, they do have gaudy beads, photographs, dolls, and other color decorations hanging above the windshield that you can spot a mile away.

Hailing a *Dolmush* is pretty much the same as hailing a taxi in Athens. First, you stand on any corner and frantically wave your arm when you see one coming. If you're lucky, it will slow down. As it approaches you, you must call out your destination loud and clear. And if you're *real* lucky, the driver will stop and pick you up.

When you get into a *Dolmush*, you have to crawl over a half dozen passengers to squeeze into one of the back seats. The process is reversed when he stops to let you off. Since there is no meter, the driver calls out how much you owe. You hand the money to a passenger who is sitting in front of you and the money is passed forward as you crawl out.

My friend, Tosun, was happy to see me. We taught together at Fairleigh Dickinson University for many years. He was a fine artist and came to Turkey each summer to paint. Each year, he would make me promise to visit him.

"I cannot believe it!" he said as he hugged me. "You, a true Greek, here in Turkey. We must celebrate!"

And celebrate we did. We celebrated until two in the morning. I dreaded the thought of making that sixteen mile trip back to my hotel in a *Dolmush*.

"Don't be foolish." Tosun said. "We will go to the edge of the Bosphorus and hire a fisherman. For two dollars, he will take you across to your hotel. It won't take more than ten minutes."

And that's exactly what we did. Naturally, Tosun haggled with a fisherman for a long time before the fisherman agreed to do it for two dollars.

Before shoving off, Tosun took me to the side and warned me, "Do not give him more than two dollars."

Feeling no pain, I climbed aboard the tiny fishing boat. The fisherman paid no attention to me when he started the engine and headed across the Bosphorus.

Put! Put! Put!

There was no moon and the stars were hidden behind an overcast sky. It was pitch black as we neared the middle of the Bosphorus.

Put! Put! Put! (silence)

Suddenly, the fisherman turned off the engine.

I asked myself, Why did he stop the engine in the middle of the Bosphorus?

I suddenly remembered Uncle Thoma's warning, *"They will cut your throat and dump your body into the Bosphorus."*

The adrenalin shot throughout my system when I sensed impending danger. I immediately assumed the *Jui-Jitsu* stance I had learned when I was a paratrooper. My feet were spread apart with my knees slightly bent, and my arms were held up in front of me. I waited for the old fisherman to make his move. But he did nothing. He just kept staring straight ahead with his back turned towards me.

What the heck is he staring at? I wondered.

I looked hard and then I saw it. A huge Russian Battleship was silently gliding past us. I looked up and the darn thing must have been fifty stories high.

I felt a little foolish standing there in my *Jui-Jitsu* stance as the fisherman started the motor again.

Put! Put! Put! Put! Put! Put!

Five minutes later, the fisherman pulled into the hotel's marina. I thanked him, handed him a ten dollar bill, and told him to keep the change.

112

Dengyou, Dengyou

I returned home from Greece on a Homeric Tours charter flight with over five hundred other passengers packed into a huge jumbo jet airplane. The passengers were Greek-Americans, like myself returning home loaded with homemade jam, olives, goat cheese, or fresh figs that were picked that morning.

I was squeezed into an aisle seat in the rear section of the airplane where all the smoke collected from the Greek chain smokers. We had just finished eating and were settling down to see a movie, when a stewardess's voice came over the loud speaker system.

"If there is a doctor aboard, please come forward. We have an emergency in the front section of the plane."

This message was repeated every few minutes. Each time, the stewardess' voice became more frantic.

After the fifth call for help, I decided to go forward to see what I could do. Although I did not have an M.D., I did have a Ph. D., and everyone at the university called me 'Doctor'. Besides, I had a lot of experience giving first aid to wounded soldiers during the war.

As I approached the front section of the plane, I saw two stewardesses struggling with a flimsy oxygen mask.

"What seems to be the trouble here?" I asked with authority.

"Oh Doctor. Thank God you're here," one of them cried out. "This man is having a heart attack!"

There was also a woman in a silk print dress, standing in the aisle and screaming, "Harry! Harry! Don't do this to me! Harry!"

When I looked at Harry, I knew I had to do something quickly. His face was a pasty-gray color, which meant he was rapidly going into shock. I immediately took charge and started to give orders, the way any good doctor would.

"Stewardess, take this woman to the back section and quiet her down."

"Yes, Doctor! Right away!"

The other stewardess asked, "Anything else, Doctor?"

"Yes, clear the passengers from these seats!"

"Yes, Doctor!"

The passengers, sitting next to Harry, immediately scrambled out of their seats.

Harry had passed out, so I turned him upside down, with his head on the floor and his feet in the air, in order to get some blood flowing into his brain.

Within minutes, color came back to his face. That's when I heard a gigantic burp! The old goat had gas in his stomach that must have been pressing against his heart, causing some discomfort. It happens to me all the time. That's why I always carry a box of *Chooz* anti-acid gum.

He opened his eyes, smiled, and said, *"Dengyou! Dengyou!"*

I spoke to him in Greek to calm him down. *"Mee stenihorieste. Imona sto strato, paratrooper, kai xero ti kano."*

He continued smiling and kept saying *"Dengyou, dengyou."*

I couldn't figure out what *"dengyou"* meant in Greek. That's when the Captain came out his flight deck to talk to me about our situation.

"Excuse me, Doctor." he said. "We are now approaching Newfoundland. We can make an emergency landing there, even though that field is not designed to handle this size plane. Unless, of course, you think that he could make it to Boston, where we could land safely."

"I'm sure we can make it to Boston," I said.

The Captain was considerably relieved and returned back to the flight deck. The old man kept saying *"Dengyou, dengyou"* and I kept wondering what it meant in Greek.

As we approached Boston, the Captain came out for another conference. Harry was now sleeping soundly, and even snoring slightly. I told the Captain that he could make it to New York without any problem. The Captain told me that they got in touch with the man's son, who happened to be a doctor at Beth Israel Hospital. The son was satisfied that his father was receiving the best care possible.

The captain also reported that there would be an ambulance waiting for him at the airport.

"Good," I said.

The plane landed safely in New York and an ambulance crew came aboard to take Harry off the plane. As he was leaving, his wife thanked me, Harry kissed my hand, and said, "*Dengyou.*"

That's when it hit me! Harry was not Greek and "*Dengyou*" was not a Greek word! Harry was Jewish and what he was saying was "*Thank you.*"

As I was leaving the plane, the fight crew and the passengers congratulated me for being there when I was needed.

Thank God, no one asked me what kind of doctor I was.

Chapter Nine

Reflections of a Greek American

A Summer Day at The Beach

Every summer, we rent a cottage for two weeks in Camp Ellis, Maine, where we vacation with the rest of the family.

In the summer of 1988, I was standing on the edge of the beach watching my nephew's six-year-old son, Adam, skipping small flat stones along the surface of the water. He was getting pretty good at it.

An old man with thin white hair unfolded a beach chair and sat closeby. We nodded to each other and focussed our attention on Adam.

"Beautiful day," I said to him.

"Yeah. Nice breeze."

After a few minutes of silence, I noticed the old man had his arm in a sling. "What happened to your arm?" I asked.

"Sprained it."

"Must be painful."

"Naw. It's okay if I don't move it."

A few more minutes of silence go by.

"Your grandson?" The old man asks.

"No. It's my nephew's son."

"Nice kid."

"Yeah. Come here often?" I ask.

"Every year."

"So do we. We usually come up in the last two weeks in August. "

"We always come in July."

"Where are you staying?"

"The Koniaris house."

"Koniaris, the optometrist. I know the house. They're from New Jersey."

"New York City," I said. "Two blocks from NYU."

"I hate New York City!"

"We love it. Where do you live in Jersey?"

"Irvington."

"Sure, Irvington. Is the Olympic Park still there?"

"Naw. Gone a long time ago. Hey? How did you know about Olympic Park?"

"Used to go there when I lived in Newark."

"You lived in Newark?" The old man's interest perked up.

"I grew up in Newark."

"You did? So did I! Where did you live?"

"West Market Street," I told him.

"That's where I lived!" The old man was now quite excited. "What school did you go to?"

"Robert Treat and then Central High. You?"

"I went there too! When did you graduate from Central?"

"In 1940."

"That's when I graduated! What did you say your name was?"

"John"

"John what?"

"Kallas"

"Johnnie Kallas?" The old man screamed and jumped out of his chair! "Johnnie Kallas! I don't believe it!"

"What's your name?" I asked, trying to figure out who this strange old man could possibly be.

"It's me, Jimmie Kafalas!"

"Jimmie Kafalas?" I screamed.

I was stunned. This old man, with white thin hair and his arm in a sling was Jimmie Kafalas. Jimmie Kafalas was my best friend all through elementary and high school. For years, we worked as ushers at the Adams Theatre and the Paramount in Newark.

He was as stunned as I was. This short stout bearded old man, watching his nephew's son, was Johnnie Kallas. The last time Jimmie saw me was 46 years ago, when I was six feet tall, weighed 125 pounds, and had all my teeth.

Thea Mariyoula

On my first trip to *Misohori* (Papa's village), I met Thea Mariyoula. Although she was then in her sixties, I was struck by her soft blue eyes and fair skin. She lived alone in a small single-room stone house overlooking the Mediterranean and was waiting to hear from her husband, Vangeli, who left Greece in 1921. Everyone in the village loved Thea Mariyoula. She was kind, gentle, and spent her entire life helping other villagers raise and care for their children.

So, this is Thea Mariyoula, I thought. She is exactly the way Papa had described her to us when we were children. Papa had often talked about Thea Mariyoula and his youngest brother, Vangeli.

Vangeli had married Mariyoula before he came to the United States with Papa and his other brothers. He promised her that he would return or send for her soon. He did neither.

After the brothers split up in Colorado, Vangeli went to South America where he vanished. Like Penelope, Mariyoula remained faithful and spent her entire life waiting for her Odesseus to return.

I recently learned that after 65 years of waiting, Thea Mariyoula received a letter from Vangeli, explaining what happened to him and begged her to forgive him. She did and died soon afterwards.

Although I never saw the letter, my cousin Niko told me what it said. Based on Niko's recollection, I wrote a theatrical peace called *AGAPI, The Greek Word For Love*, which is reproduced on the next three pages.

The piece was written in loving memory of Thea Mariyoula.

119

AGAPI
The Greek Word For Love

By John Kallas

Time: 1985

Place: A small village of tiny white washed houses with red-tiled rooftops, nestled on a mountainside, at the southern tip of the Peloponnesian Peninsula, 4,000 feet above the Mediterranean.

The single-room home of Mariyoula is sparsely furnished. Hanging on the wall next to the door is the semi-round tin can that holds the household water that must be fetched each day from the village well.

A small wooden table stands next to it with a large porcelain wash basin on it.

A large open window looks out at the light blue sea whose horizon blends with the light blue sky. The light curtains dance gently in the constant mountain breeze.

In the center of the room is a large wooden table with a few wooden chairs set around it.

Hanging in the corner of the room is an icon of The Virgin Mother Mary illuminated by the flickering flame of a candelli hanging from the ceiling.

The only other object hanging on the wall is a large oval-shaped ornate frame containing a large faded, tinted photograph of a young couple, taken in 1920. The young man in the photograph is sitting in a stuffed chair holding a stiff derby hat in the crook of his arm. His stern face is adorned with heavy eyebrows and a large handlebar moustache.

Standing next to him in the photo is a sixteen-year-old beautiful, petite girl with large eyes and thin lips. Her thick blond hair is piled high in a huge bun on top of her head.

THEA MARIYOULA, now a seventy-five-year-old woman, dressed in black, with her head covered with a black shawl, enters holding a letter. Although she is old, her smooth white skin still reflects her gentle and dignified beauty.

She trembles with excitement as she lights a kerosene lamp.

THEA MARIYOULA

Panayia mou... Panayia mou... He is alive. He IS alive! Panayia mou!

She holds the envelope up to the light to read the handwriting on the sealed envelope which is filled with bright-colored foreign stamps.

THEA MARIYOULA

It's his handwriting. I know his handwriting. After all these years, his handwriting is still the same. Panayia mou... He is alive. My Vangeli is still alive.

With her old trembling fingers, she carefully opens the sealed envelope and slowly pulls out the folded letter, written on light blue paper, and gently opens it to read.

THEA MARIYOULA

My dearest wife, Mariyoula,

I pray to God that this letter finds you alive and in good health.

I also pray to Panayia to help me find the right words to say what I have to say.

It is difficult to tell you what happened. Perhaps it is best that I start at the beginning.

When I left you and went to America to work with my brothers in the coal mines, I told you that I would come back a rich man with lots of money. I told you then that it would take a year, two years at the most, and you told me that you would wait, even if it took forever.

The two years we worked in the coal mines were worse than being in hell itself. I am sure that my brothers told you how bad it was when they came back home.

When Stavros was killed in the explosion, we left the mines. As you know Elias and Stathie stayed in America, Niko went to South Africa. Polihroni and Paraskava came back home with less money than they had when they left Greece. I could not come back, not like that. So, I went to Brazil in South America.

Working in the swamps and jungles in Brazil was worse than digging coal in America. In a little while I got malaria and almost died with fever. A nurse, a Spanish woman, slowly brought me back to life.

When I left the hospital, I went to live with this woman. I was still very weak and she continued to care for me. She bore me a son, and a daughter after that.

We then got married, moved to a large city, opened a small grocery store, and worked in it eighteen hours a day. We never took time off to rest.

We had seven children. The years went by so quickly. My children and business left me no time to think about the past. It is not possible that sixty years passed by so quickly. But, they did.

Please forgive me. If you do, I will know and I will die in peace.

Your husband, Vangeli.

THEA MARIYOULA slowly folds the letter and puts it back into the envelope. She presses it close to her fragile body. She gets up from the table and wedges the envelope into the edge of the framed photograph. She gently touches the face of the man in the photograph.

She then slowly walks to the icon of the Virgin Mother Mary, crosses herself while she leans over and kisses the icon.

THEA MARIYOULA

I forgive him, God. Please let him die in peace.

Thanks...

To all my friends who made it a joy for me to work on this project.

To my performer friends for their music, singing, and reading that made these stories come alive.

Jimmy Dukas   **Vangeli Fampas**
Anna Paidoussi   **Loukas Skipitaris**

To my fellow writers for their literary assistance and encouragement.

Eleni Paidoussi and **Regina Pagoulatou**

To my friends for their editing. **Michael McCullough, Susan McAuley,** and **Fran A. Pappas.**

To my dearest friends for their artistic advice and help.

Jim Markowich and **Sandy Mayer.**

To **Warren Kliewer** and **Michelle LaRue** who suggested I write this book.

To my literary agent **Knox Burger** for his expert guidance and to **Tom Kemnitz,** my publisher, for being my friend and a true Grecophile.

A very special thanks to my wife, **Judith C. Kallas** for her editorial help and honest criticism.

And to all the organizations that have sponsored the theatrical presentation of the stories.

The Greek Writers Guild of America

The Metropolitan Greek Chorale

The Players

The Grecian Heritage Foundation "ORPHEUS"

The Cornelia Street Cafe.

To all of you "Dengyou! Dengyou!"

About The Author

JOHN KALLAS, a son of Greek parents, is steeped in the immigrant experience. As a boy growing up in Newark he shined shoes, sold newspapers, and taught his father to speak English.

As a young man he joined the 82nd Airborne Division during World War II, jumped into Normandy the night before D Day and subsequently survived the Battle of the Bulge and the jump across the Rhine River.

After the war, he attended night school at Fairleigh Dickinson University, where he received a B.A. degree in fine arts and later at New York University where he earned M.A. and Ph.D. degrees. He rose from the ranks of a junior draftsman at Western Electric in Kearny to become an electronics and computer designer at Bell Telephone Laboratories.

He retired from Bell Telephone Laboratories to teach at New York University and later became a professor at Fairleigh Dickinson University, where he recently retired as chairman of the Microcomputers in Education Department to concentrate on his playwriting.

He has participated in the Actor's Studio Playwright Lab, where he wrote *Infinity*. He also founded the Manhattan Playwrights Unit and was chairman of the board of directors for the Greek Theatre of New York.

Recently he was accepted as a *Man of The Theatre* member by The Players, and is presently an active member of the Greek Writers Guild of America and on the board of directors of The Metropolitan Greek Chorale.

A number of his plays have been produced in New York. They include: *Mispossesed, Infinity, The Maniati, Pandora, Santacom,* and *The Corporal.*